IT'S
HERE. . .
SOMEWHERE!

Alice Fulton
and Pauline Hatch

IT'S
HERE . . .
SOMEWHERE!

Writer's
Digest
Books

Cincinnati, Ohio

Illustrations by Shunichi Yamamoto,
Great Western Promotions.

Library of Congress Cataloging-in-Publication Data

Fulton, Alice, 1949-
  It's here. . .somewhere!

  Bibliography: p.
  Includes index.
  1. Home economics. 2. Dwellings. I. Hatch, Pauline, 1946-
  II. Title.
TX303.F85 1985   640   85-20221
ISBN 0-89879-186-3

Book design by Alice Mauro.

Pauline and Alice dedicate this book to Pauline and Alice (even though they probably should dedicate it to their husbands and kids!). When the rest of the world wondered and doubted, they continued to believe in their ability to see It's Here. . .Somewhere! *to a successful end!*

Contents

Preface

"It's here, *somewhere*," is what most of you probably say at least once a day when you can't find something in your home. Certainly the two of us used to find ourselves saying it all too often at the end of all too many unsuccessful searches. Not that our homes were dirty, or that we were lazy. We cleaned regularly and worked hard all the time, but locating our families' assorted possessions was like trying to find the proverbial needle in the haystack.

We're convinced that you're trying at least as hard as we did, yet still suffer from some degree of clutter at your house. Like us, you've probably read and heard lots of advice, some helpful, some not. After long experience, we think we really do have some solutions, and we'd like to share them with you. In short, we've come to the conclusion that simplifying your home will go a long way toward helping you run your household—and your family life—more smoothly. That's what this book is about, and we hope it will be as helpful to you as the techniques we describe have been for us.

Acknowledgments

Special thanks to:

Don Aslett for sharing his time, talents, and practical counsel with us.

Budge Wallis, for listening to us over lunch and for his gracious hand-delivery of our manuscript to Writer's Digest Books.

Howard I. Wells III, for his wisdom and patience.

Willa Speiser, for her professional insight as our editor, who helped us turn our thoughts and ideas into clear, written concepts.

The staff at Writer's Digest Books, for their commitment to quality and for their ability to help us turn our desires and dreams into reality.

Introduction

Belongings have a nasty way of proliferating: The more space you have, the more things you acquire to fill that space. And suddenly your home, however spacious it may once have seemed, is crowded, disorganized, and not nearly as welcoming as it once was.

In fact, space is at a premium for more and more of us these days. There's less of it to go around, and what there is gets more expensive by the day. With the costs of new housing constantly on the rise, and the cost of heating and maintaining older homes increasing too, most people can't afford much, if any, "extra" room—and certainly can't afford any wasted space.

The space crunch notwithstanding, we're by no means planning to suggest to you, anywhere in this book, that you divest yourself of your belongings—not the ones that matter, anyway. What we *do* suggest is that you simplify, then organize, your entire home. It's not enough to shuffle things around from this shelf to that drawer; getting rid of the overload is what makes the difference. Once that's done, just about *any* organizing system will work and last, whether that system is based on which member of the family owns what, what kinds of activities items are used for, or what letter of the alphabet an item's name starts with.

HOW DO YOU START?

The key to this not-so-mysterious process of organization is to evaluate everything you own. Does it deserve to share your living space?

Do this evaluation with an eye to creating two groups—"keepers" and "tossers." Keepers are what make your home *yours*, but combined with tossers, they equal overload. Get rid of your tossers, and you've eliminated your overload. Basically, this means that you'll need to choose between what you know you'll use (and a few things you love, too, even if you never use them) and what you don't use.

Once you've gotten past this step, good organization will follow almost automatically.

We think a room-by-room approach to both the choosing and using steps is the way to go. Not everyone has the same kinds or numbers of rooms, but we all know that kitchens, baths, bedrooms, the family room, and that infamous storage area, each offer their own special kinds of clutter and potential organization.

To help you approach your house as efficiently and painlessly as possible, we've organized this book by room and area. That way, if there's a room you *don't* have a problem with, you can simply skip the chapter that deals with it. Better still, thinking about the jobs one room at a time makes the overall task seem much less overwhelming, and thus, much more do-able.

Will All This REALLY Do Any Good?

You bet, because this isn't the usual material on organizing. We don't teach organization, so you won't find lots of clever organization tips in this book—we've left this to the other two million writers. We teach streamlining, or unloading the overload. We believe the reason that you, and millions of readers like you, haven't achieved permanent order and control of your interior spaces is that you've been trying to organize too much stuff. We believe in clear surfaces rather than "organized" surfaces. We say get rid of everything you don't like, use, need, want, or have room for. What's left will be quality keepers and lots of empty spaces. Put the two together and you'll have your own brand of lasting organization.

We're professional consultants who've helped thousands of homemakers streamline their homes. The feedback is overwhelming . . . in every case, unloading the overload was what they needed, not using any particular organization techniques.

This streamlining system is what makes us unique—what makes our streamlining system unique is that it works . . . it REALLY will do you good.

What we're about to tell you *is* a lot of work, initially. But if you keep up the system and adopt streamlining as your homemaking method, you'll never have to go through this initial unloading again. And yes, it will make a tremendous difference in your home and in your life. Here are just some of the benefits.

MORE SPACE

We do indeed live in an affluent and material-oriented society. Radio, television, magazines, even books—all tell us that possessing *things* makes us successful, important, attractive, and happy. But few of us have the space, mental or physical, to accommodate all that we've been inspired to collect. It's inevitable that you, like the two of us, have acquired more than you need. And in the midst of that clutter, it's not easy to find the things that count (and we don't mean just material belongings). The solution: Find what's worth keeping, and discard the rest.

Let's look in a typical kitchen gadget drawer, for example—that is, if we can get it open past the heads of the handmixer beaters and two wire whisks. We discover not only the beaters and whisks, but four potato peelers, two ladles (one of them rusty), several dull paring knives, and three pancake turners (a plastic one, a metal one in good condition, and another metal one with the plastic handle broken off). This isn't all. More digging unearths two tangled electric frypan cords, a butcher knife, two sets of measuring cups (one plastic, the other dented metal), and two sets of measuring spoons. Wedged in among all these "necessities" we find five cocktail forks, one gooey, rusty can opener, four little plastic pop bottle lids, three rubber spatulas (two with ragged edges), and a bunch (we've quit counting) of Popsicle sticks.

This drawer definitely needs simplifying. We begin by discarding one wire whisk and three potato peelers. If you ever manage to round up four people who will peel potatoes simultaneously, you can borrow three extra peelers from a neighbor—who is certain to have them. The rusty ladle and dull paring knives don't deserve space in any drawer, so out they go, too. Sharpen the best knives, and put them aside for now; we'll find a place for them later. No one should have to use a pancake turner with a broken handle, and there are already two good ones, so why keep the third? The frypan cords—assuming they work and are for different pans—should be stored with their respective pans, with the cords wound and secured. If space is a problem, keep one set of measuring spoons and cups, storing them with the mixer beaters. Since a collection of five cocktail forks isn't a complete set, but is something of a space waster, we suggest tossing them. And get rid of the rusty can opener at the same time, then replace it with a new one. Four plastic pop bottle lids, although small, add their bit to the confusion; for simplicity's sake, group them together, perhaps in a small plastic bag. (This goes for all little, like items—keep control of them by grouping them in small containers.) Finally, keep the good rubber

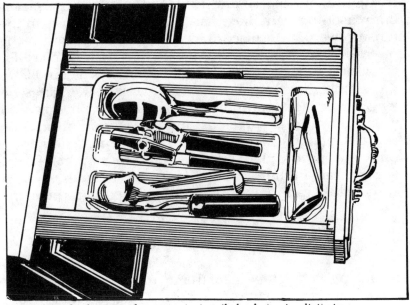

Discarding duplicate and worn-out utensils leads to simplicity in a kitchen gadget drawer.

spatula; throw out the two ragged ones.

Obviously, this simplifying technique will create far more space in any kitchen drawer. It's enough to make you think more kindly of almost any amount of kitchen storage space, since you'll very likely discover that you're not nearly as short of space as you thought. In fact, simplifying on a large scale may even convince you that your house is the perfect size for your family after all.

NO MORE CLUTTER

After you organize what is left after simplifying, things tend to stay where you've put them. And that will reduce clutter and confusion, create order, and give you control of space and things. When you need something, you'll go right to it.

Back to the advice to "organize your home by having a place for everything and keeping everything in its place." That's all very well, but it doesn't go far enough. When we thought about places and things to put in those places, our reasoning went like this: "The place for junk is in the junk drawer . . . the place for clothes is in the closet . . . the place for mixing bowls is in the kitchen . . ." The place-for-everything adage is too broad and general as it stands. Do the simplifying first, however, and it works. Things no longer have vague or random placement in our homes, and we no longer waste precious time "treasure hunting." Because simplifying left us with fewer items to organize, finding a specific place and keeping things in their specific place has become easier. Under these circumstances, even a child can maintain almost any space in the home.

A BETTER-LOOKING HOME

Managing belongings goes hand in hand with owning them. Part of the management is making decisions about the purpose of things and their place in the home. Constant decision making can bog you down, though. If you don't know where to put something, or if you're faced with a number of homeless items, you're likely to let each one sit where it is, or cram it in somewhere that it shouldn't go. Years of living with clutter and shuffling have taught us that clutter isn't charming, pretty, or restful, no matter how attractive each component of it is. But when everything has a proper place and is put there, each item looks its best. And that makes the entire house look better.

MORE EFFICIENT LAYOUT

Spaces that hold too much stuff are not only ugly but inefficient as well. For example, a front hall closet holds coats much better if the vacuum cleaner, golf clubs, sleeping bags, and board games are removed from it. And kitchen countertops will invite you, graciously rather than demandingly, to cook or bake if they are free of the toaster, electric can opener, blender, canisters, coffee or wheat grinder, and food processor.

You are probably muttering with some hostility, "Oh sure, sure . . . so *where* do I put all this stuff?" Well, remember that simplifying not only assigns items to appropriate places within your home but also to charity boxes and trash bags. Trust us: there will be a proper place for everything that's left after simplifying.

EASIER MAINTENANCE

If you simplify, you will have a home you can be proud of without spending all your time keeping it up. Simplifying isn't magic, and no little fairies will do last night's dishes or mop the floors, but there *will* be less to do. Back to the kitchen counters, for example: Removing the items that used to sit on the countertop automatically eliminates that constant "wipe and shine" routine. Because appliances are out of the way of spills and spatters, they stay cleaner longer and require less attention, and you'll find the counters themselves will be easier to keep clean because there will be little or nothing to remove when wiping up. Another benefit of keeping your countertops empty is that kitchen helpers can clearly tell when they are finished with the cleanup.

SAVINGS IN TIME AND ENERGY

Simplifying leaves you with less to take care of, and organizing gives what's left a place all its own. Having fewer possessions to sort, clean, fold, put away, dust, or shuffle saves you time and energy. You'll also spend less time looking for all the lost what-have-yous. (We can't count all the times we arrived late and angry at a meeting because of misplaced car keys, kids' shoes, coats, and so on.)

In preparing material for this book and our seminars, we've kept detailed records of time spent on routine chores before and after simplifying. The results are convincing.

TASK	BEFORE	AFTER
Dusting a 2,000-sq.-ft. home	35 minutes	15-17 minutes

The savings is dramatic, and came about because surfaces needing dusting were clear of clutter. There was no more need to move the clutter, or dust it.

Now if 35 minutes for dusting doesn't seem like much to you, consider this: If you dust twice a week, the time spent is 70 minutes a week. Multiply this 70 minutes by the 52 weeks in a year, and you spend 3,640 minutes, or over 60 hours a year, just dusting.

TASK	BEFORE	AFTER
Vacuuming the floors and stairs; 2,000-sq.-ft. home	40 minutes	25 minutes

Again, the time is almost cut in half, thanks to not having to move or navigate around clutter.

If you vacuum three times a week, the total time comes to 120 minutes, or two hours. Multiply this two hours by 52 weeks, and you'll find that you spend 104 hours a year vacuuming.

TASK	BEFORE	AFTER
Laundry for a family of nine, with children under 14	14-16 loads a week	9-10 loads a week

Everyone owns clothing he or she never wears. And yet for one reason or another, especially if the family includes children, much of this "never wear" clothing ends up in the laundry. Sixteen loads of wash each week, at 15 minutes for washing and 20 minutes for drying, per load, takes 560 minutes a week to do. Multiply this figure by 52 and you get 29,120 minutes a year, or more than 485 hours. That's almost 21 days a year on laundry!

PEACE OF MIND

No matter where you spend your day, your home is the key to your world. And even if you do something other than homemaking for a living, your home is also your business. If you aren't managing it well, everyone suffers, but *you* suffer the most—from low self-esteem, from anger at the constant mess, from frustration over not being in control of things. When the causes of these negative feelings are eliminated, you'll feel a lot better about yourself, and that improvement will be reflected in everything you do.

Consider the benefits in just one area—hospitality. No more qualms, psalms, or sweaty palms over an unexpected visitor seeing your house in its "real-life" state. No more frustration and fatigue when you're preparing for expected guests. No more envy and depression when comparing your house with your neighbor's. Having more space, order, a better-looking home, and efficient rooms that are easier to care for will take care of all that.

We challenge you to put our "simplify first" ideas to the test. Be open-minded, follow the instructions, and use the concepts faithfully for 21 days (it's been said that that is how long it takes to break a bad habit and establish a good one). We're sure you'll all reap the benefits we've described—and probably a few more.

Basic Training

This book is based on a series of basic ideas and steps that we've tested in hundreds of homes. We've kept in touch with all the homemakers we've worked with directly, so we know that the rules still apply—and work—at their homes. The rules will work for you, too, no matter what size your family is, how high or low your income, or whether you live in the city, the country, or the suburbs.

Now let's take a look at what these basics are.

THE LAW OF HOUSEHOLD PHYSICS

The Law of Household Physics says, "Only so much will fit into one space and still let you retain order and control." You can't cram 3 square feet of stuff into a 1½-square-foot drawer and expect that drawer to look nice, stay looking nice after you've plowed through it looking for something, and keep everything in bounds.

Usually, the amount of space available is fixed; it's the amount of stuff that's variable. That's why you must eliminate some items if you want to establish permanent control of your spaces. That means learning to live within the limits of your physical space, or facing the constant frustration of knowing you've lost control of that space.

THE LAW OF HOUSEHOLD ECOLOGY

It's easy to abide by the Law of Household Physics if you live according to the Law of Household Ecology: When something new comes in, something else must go out. This keeps a balance between things and space. When you get a new coat, get rid of an old, tired, less stylish one; stop giving space to it, hoping it will come back in style. And even if it did come back in style, which is perfectly possible, it still wouldn't look good because of the worn elbows, frayed pocket edges, and saggy seat. When you get a new ballpoint pen, get rid of the old, dead one. If you've decided disposable razors suit your needs, discard the dull-bladed, tired electric razor. In short, keep a manageable balance by taking out when you bring in.

THE LAW OF REDUCTION

Overload reduces the amount of living space in any home. The more things, the less space; reduce the things, and you automatically expand the space. We've talked to many people who said that after simplifying, they found not only order and control, but what seemed to be a "new" home as well. Many who once complained about a too-small home are now content with their existing space.

THREE PRICE TAGS

When you're considering your belongings, assign the title of "keeper" fairly. Try to remember that everything has three price tags. The first price is the one paid at the time of purchase. After the item is brought into the home, you pay a second price—in space. Everything you own, whether it's a bobby pin or a rolling pin, takes up *some* space. The third price is the cost of maintenance: Almost everything you own must be maintained in some way. So look at your current possessions and at any purchases you may consider in the future, and ask yourself if you really want to pay three prices. Often, the initial monetary price turns out to be the smallest of the three.

SURFACE MESS VS. SURFACE NEATNESS

There is an important distinction between surface mess and surface neatness. Surface mess is what you have when you're in the kitchen canning peaches and fixing supper at the same time. It's what you have when every available surface in the office is holding stacks of reports, files, and notes while you're trying to meet a deadline. Surface mess isn't a problem if everything in that mess has a specific place to go, and can be put there quickly and easily. Surface mess is a normal result of living.

Surface neatness is a problem, however. When you have surface neatness, you're likely to be doing the household shuffle—moving items from place to place—far too often. It's a phony lifestyle, and one that too many people are living. It's neat on top only, and temporarily at best. It's what you have when you know you're having company and you hope they don't open the wrong door or cupboard. It's what you have (if you're lucky) when you don't know you're having company and you hope the drop-ins don't open the

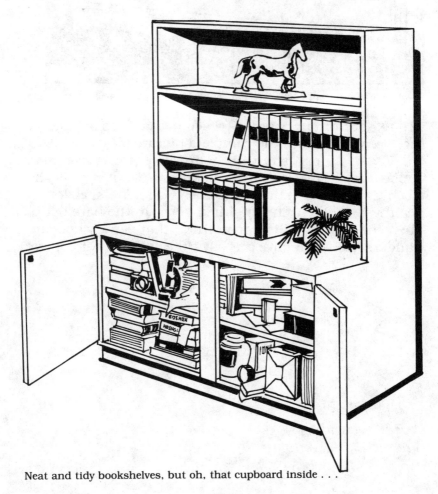

Neat and tidy bookshelves, but oh, that cupboard inside . . .

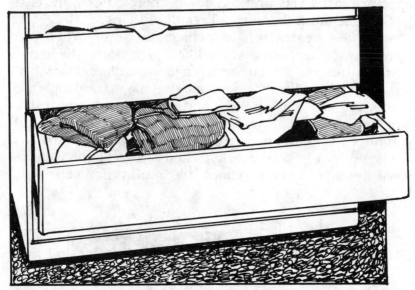

Drawers are part of a home's skeleton, where clutter control is essential.

wrong door or cupboard. Surface neatness is self-defeating, because it isn't the complete picture.

The real story is in your home's skeleton—its closets, cupboards, and drawers. What those are like tells the truth about what shape a home is in. The skeleton is healthy if it has been simplified down to the bare bones. Then there will be little or nothing that can escape and wander, and you'll have an easy time with clutter control.

According to the Law of Reduction, when you decrease the number of things, you'll visually as well as physically expand your space.

Take
Eight Giant Steps

Okay. You're convinced that simplifying and sorting out your family's belongings really *will* make a big difference in your day-to-day life. But you're not quite sure just what is involved. Determination is a key factor, of course, but there are also eight distinct steps. Here they are:

STEP 1
Prepare Your Family

Tell *all* members of the household what you're planning to do, how you will do it, and why you want to do it. Make sure everyone understands what they can expect from you while you're digging out from under the overload. And explain what you will expect from them.

STEP 2
Collect Containers

This may not be a new concept, but it definitely works. You'll need four big containers per room—large boxes, heavy-duty trash bags, even big brown grocery bags. Label one "someplace else" for any keeper that doesn't belong in the room you're working in. Label another "charity" for usable things that you no longer want anywhere in the house. Label a third "garbage." (It's only fair to be discriminating when you load charity bags—much of the stuff people send to charity really belongs in the garbage. When you drop your donations off, be sure to ask for your tax-deduction receipt.) Label the last container "to file." You'll find filable material in all parts of your home. (For example, Alice found her family's life insurance papers in a master bedroom dresser drawer.) The "to file" box will catch everything from the aforementioned insurance papers, birth

Use containers such as these to gain order and control during the streamlining process.

certificates, the hot-water-heater warranty, the first essay your eighteen-year-old ever wrote, and even newspaper and magazine clippings. Group all filable material together, but don't deal with it until your entire home is finished; then you'll have enough time and mental energy.

Don't take time to deal with the "someplace else" containers until you've sorted out the whole house. You'll get sidetracked otherwise. Yes, you'll be accumulating lots of these boxes, and you will wonder where everything will go. But remember, while you're adding up "someplace else" boxes, you are also emptying space. The someplace else things will eventually "melt" into empty spaces.

To avoid confusion, tie the charity and garbage bags differently—maybe twist-ties on the garbage and yarn on the charity. And do yourself a favor: Don't allow anyone to open a closed bag or box. They will undo every good thing you've accomplished by playing the "I can use this" game.

Now for the small containers. There's no set number. Just collect lots of shoeboxes, plastic refrigerator contain-

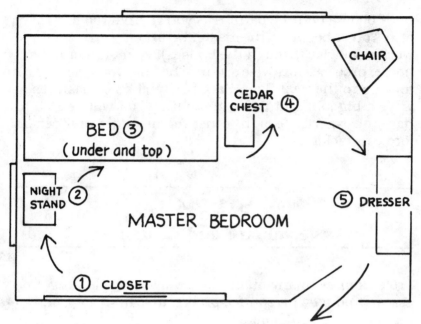

Begin simplifying in the master bedroom, starting at the closet and moving clockwise from one area to the next.

ers, cottage cheese and margarine tubs, drawstring bags (see our Streamlined Drawstring Bag Construction idea in the Back-of-the-Book Bonus section), and so on. You'll use them to organize drawers, cupboards, and closets.

STEP 3
Work in a Clockwise Pattern

Work in a clockwise pattern around the perimeter of each room, bringing your four big containers with you. Working like this enables you to see where you've been and know where you're going. This method prevents time-wasting distractions. If you are in a bedroom, start at the closet. Deal with *each* item you come to as you progress around the room, assigning things to the four containers. (Moving in a clockwise pattern is a good technique when cleaning, too.)

Follow a definite pattern as you go from room to room, also. You've begun in the master bedroom, and from there work clockwise through the house. If yours is a multilevel home, proceed clockwise around the floor you're on before moving to the next floor. Save the kitchen for last. It's always a big job, and time-consuming. You will be glad to have the experience of the other rooms under your belt before you tackle it.

STEP 4
Evaluate and Assign

Professionals in any business are always evaluating processes, products, personnel, procedures, inventory, and so on. A professional homemaker does the same thing. (And a professional homemaker isn't necessarily a full-time one—just one who's very good and very thorough at that job.) Think about *where* things are used and *how often*, as well as *when* you use them and *why*. Answers to these questions determine appropriate resting places for everything. The shoeshine kit is a good case in point: If it's used often, then it deserves convenient storage space. And if it is used in the kitchen, then it should be stored there, rather than in the bathroom, bedroom, or basement. Canning equipment is another example: Although usually used in the kitchen, it is used only seasonally, so it doesn't deserve prime kitchen space. It would be better to store it in some out-of-the-way place and take it out only when needed.

Have you ever thought about what you want on the top shelf of your front hall closet or what you specifically want in the bottom drawer of your bathroom vanity? Or what you definitely want in the drawer by the refrigerator? Start thinking this way: Assign specific purposes to all spaces in your home and then allow them to fulfill that function and none other.

22

STEP 5
Ask the Right Questions

This is a key point in making decisions about storage. Before storing anything, ask yourself the following questions for each item in each room.

√Do I like it?
√Do I use it?
√Do I want it?
√Do I need it?
√Do I have room for it?

Even if you answer yes to the first four questions, if you answer no to the last one, you may need to reevaluate. The key to gaining permanent control of your home is to work *with* your space, not against it. Remember the Law of Household Physics: You only have so much space, and sometimes there just is not room for all that you like, use, want, or need. It may come down to a choice between lots of stuff and little control or little stuff and lots of control. Remember that keepers *plus* tossers create overload. Keepers by themselves don't do that—they add individuality to your home.

Be ruthlessly realistic when deciding what to toss and what to keep, and think quality over quantity. Do you really like that all-cotton tablecloth that needs ironing each time it's used? Do you really use that heating pad with the short in the cord? Do you really need those 1969 wooden skis that you haven't been on in fifteen years? Do you really want that white straw purse with the cracked bamboo handle? Using all five questions on everything you own will make letting go of things easier, "buy" you space, and help you stop shuffling things around, so get into the habit of thinking about your things. Make these questions and their answers part of your lifestyle.

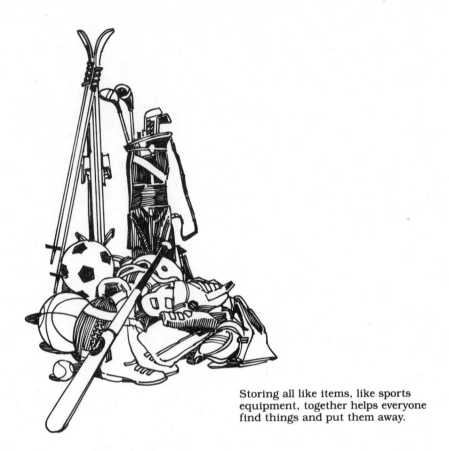

Storing all like items, like sports equipment, together helps everyone find things and put them away.

STEP 6
Group and Store Like Items Together

Again, this isn't a new idea, but it's very important. Doing this will put logic into the placement of things.

The practice of grouping and storing like items together has several advantages. First, you will have only one place to look for things. Second, finding and putting away becomes easier as you put a stop to the household treasure-hunt pattern. Finally, grouping and storing like items together is a great time, energy, and nerve saver. It lets you know what's missing, and what's duplicated. It buys you space and it creates order.

This rule includes storing seasonal items, such as snowsuits, boots, and gloves together—and out of the way when they're out of season. It's wasteful to give these things prime space all year round. (When finished streamlining each room and area of your home, you'll be ready to put once-and-for-all order into your storage area—whether this is the basement, a separate room, or a garage corner. We discuss this in Chapter 17.)

STEP 7
Use Memento Boxes

There is a place in our homes and lives for the sentimental. Author and household-management expert Daryl Hoole says that place is a treasure or memento box. A grocery-store cardboard orange or apple box with a lid makes a good starter box—each family member should have his or her own. We suggest you eventually invest in a quality container—perhaps even one that's custom-made, with hinged lid. This should be as nice as the contents, an heirloom in itself.

Baby books, scrapbooks, photo albums, ancestral heirlooms, vacation mementos, a last doll or treasured toy, and baby booties are some contents suggestions. A large manila envelope (one for each child) could hold school report cards and selected school papers.

Obviously, this is not something the neighbor children are allowed into. A memento box is not a toy box, but rather a central holding spot for the child's personal treasures. Memento-box items mean nothing to the neighbors; thus, there is a strong chance these mementos will be abused. We suggest assigning this box to the child's closet shelf, where it'll be available, but just enough out of reach to ensure protection.

As a child moves from one stage of development to another, his idea of "treasures" changes. One month he's into Popsicle sticks, two months later his treasure is his sticker collection, and eventually his interest moves from stickers to his school autograph book. Note that the child's contributions will also share space in this box with your additions—the baby album, first rattle, bronzed baby booties, and so on. So, to prevent this box from expanding to the size of a mini-storage shed, have the child occasionally reevaluate the box's contents, discard some things, and make room for new "treasures." This is excellent experience: it's a lucky child who learns early on to live the Laws of Household Physics and Ecology.

A memento box solves the problem of storing sentimental treasures.

Overloaded and out-of-control space is exasperating.

Enjoy empty space and the feeling of control.

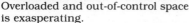

STEP 8
Enjoy the Empty Space

Don't let empty space make you nervous. It does take some adjusting to, since it's almost always a radical change. But give empty spaces a chance for at least twenty-one days, and you'll end up loving them even more than filled spaces. Empty space is a basic part of your home; it's peaceful, airy, calming, even beautiful. Work to keep it; make it a homemaking standard. (Just as a bathroom isn't completely finished until the chrome is shiny, a room isn't completely finished until some spaces are empty.)

Now that you know what *to* do, here are a few *don'ts*.

√Don't be afraid to throw things away.

√Don't feel guilty about throwing things away—or wanting to.

√Don't keep anything that is broken and cannot be repaired—or that in your heart of hearts you have no intention of repairing.

√Don't allow well-meaning givers to intimidate you into keeping things you really don't want to keep. Many of us worry that so-and-so will "just die" if we get rid of his offering. Experts agree that no one dies when we toss out something someone has given to us.

And remember, this major clearing out is a one-shot experience. You'll never have to dig out like this again, because if you adopt these steps as part of your lifestyle, your home will never be overloaded again. Let these eight steps become your homemaking standards, and change your life.

4

On Your Mark, Get Set, . . .

There are some things you and your family should know before you start your household revolution. The most important thing is to realize in advance that it won't happen overnight or without some strain.

● Expect to be tired at the end of each simplifying session. This is hard physical work.

● Brace yourself for some family resistance. Bad habits die hard, and we've seen many families threatened by this change in their lifestyle. They can cope fairly well with the picking-up and putting-away, but the throwing- and giving-away causes anger and sometimes resistance. After all, their identities, personalities, and very lives are intertwined with their belongings. Don't let them wear you down . . . stick to your guns.

● Count on experiencing some emotional strain. Misplaced sentiment, for example, can make it hard to let go of things. One friend of ours, whom we helped dig out a closet, was giving precious space to over fifty pounds of stained, stretched-out, faded layette items. She knew she needed the space those things were taking up; she knew most of those things were beyond ever looking nice again; she knew she'd be able to replace them if she needed to. But none of that made discarding those things any easier. She cried, but once she had discarded the stuff, she was glad she had.

● Part of your preparation will probably involve an attitude overhaul. Basically, it's attitudes about belongings, not the items themselves, that cause overloaded houses. These attitudes can restrict, even cripple you, as you struggle to keep order in the home. For instance, if you're firmly convinced you can't get along without your 1961 Junior Prom dress, your square-toed platform shoes, and your double-knit floor-length skirts, then you won't give them up. And if you won't give them up, then you'll continue to live and struggle with overloaded closets.

We've helped many people simplify their homes, and without exception, this is what we heard: "I can't throw that

31

away, I might need it someday," or "My mother (or sister, or husband, or neighbor) would just die if I got rid of this!" Then there's: "We're gonna get this fixed someday," and the real zinger, "We're saving this for so-and-so." (Believe us, so-and-so will be better off if you don't save for him.) If you are thinking or saying any of these things, an attitude overhaul may be in order.

Simplifying your home involves lots of good changes, so be flexible enough to try something different. Professionals in any field are always looking for a better way to do things—they're frequently changing this arrangement or that system. Instead of saying, "How can you have an empty shelf?" or "There's not enough room anywhere else!" or "There's no other way to do it," be professional in your outlook, and give yourself the freedom to experiment and make changes.

An attitude overhaul will cut your streamlining time by two-thirds and save you energy. Case in point: The kitchen of a 1,950-square-foot tri-level home took nine-and-a-half hours to simplify (and the homemaker had emptied all the cupboards and drawers before we arrived!) because much time was spent talking her out of things and into new ideas. We not only had to deal with her belongings, but her preconceptions and closed mind as well. In contrast, the kitchen of a 2,000-square-foot ranch house took three hours to simplify. And these three hours included the time it took us to help the homemaker unload all her drawers and cupboards. This woman was open-minded and receptive to all our basic principles and steps; all we had to deal with was her *things*. So speed the project up and save lots of stress and energy; have an open mind and a positive attitude about the changes.

• Not only does the getting rid of items cause stress, the decision making does, too. Brace yourself for it. Simplifying requires hundreds of decisions, all made by you. When we were helping one homemaker simplify her master bedroom, we found an assortment of more than seventy-five greeting cards in her bottom dresser drawer. She had to decide what to do with every Mother's Day card, birthday card, and all the get-well cards she'd received for her 1954 tonsillectomy. After looking at about twenty-five cards, she put five or six in her memento box, picked up the rest, and said, "What's the point in keeping all these?" Then she dumped the whole bunch into the trash. She had learned an important concept or two from this exercise: You can't afford to give valuable space to nonessential duplicates, and finding appropriate places for all potential keepers causes you to be very selective.

By making decisions about everything you own, you develop a new perspective, and a firm resolve not to get overloaded ever again. Our card-collecting friend now thinks twice before she stores newly received greeting cards. Most of the time they go in the garbage after she's savored them for a few days. Her few keeper cards never end up in the bottom dresser drawer anymore; they now have an appropriate home in her memento box.

• Brace yourself for the temporary mess that digging out will cause. You'll have little trouble with the charity and garbage items, because they'll have instant places to go. It's the accumulation of "someplace else" things that will create the mess and cause some irritation. To avoid this, set aside one room (or even a large closet or space along one wall) as a temporary catchall for these "someplace else" bags and boxes. We call it a *temporary* catchall because it will be; each and every "someplace else" item will be dealt with by the time your simplifying is over. Eventually all the "someplace else" stuff (only keepers, remember) will fit into the empty spaces you've left in each room. So be patient with this mess. It's only temporary.

• Be aware, also, that some of your acquaintances may greet your bubbling enthusiasm over your new homemaking style with disinterest. Don't let this hurt or discourage you. Disinterest, even mild ridicule, are common reactions people have when they sense progress or success in another's life. And you'll definitely be progressing and suc-

JANUARY				Goal: *streamline house*		
SUN	**MON**	**TUES**	**WED**	**THURS**	**FRI**	**SAT**
		1 *holiday*	2	3	4	5 *Streamline M.Bdrm (baked chicken)*
6	7	8	9	10	11 ←*Streamline* 7–10 *bath*	12 *Streamline→ guest rm (la sagne)*
13	14 ←*Streamline* 7–10 *Kids rm (pot roast)*	15 7–10 *hall closet (spaghetti)*	16 7–10 *family rm (fish/chips)*	17 7–10 *Kitchen (Soup+salad)*	18 →7–9 *Kitchen (go out)*	19
20	21	22	23	24	25	26 *Streamline storage (hamburgers)*
27	28	29	30	31		

Plan ahead—clear the decks to concentrate on simplifying. (This example could accommodate a working woman. The idea would easily adapt to a full-time homemaker if the notations for evening hours, shown during the weekdays, were removed.)

ceeding as you take control of your physical surroundings. Just be prepared for this reaction, chalk it up to human nature, and continue in your enthusiasm for the project.

● Simplifying goes more smoothly if there has been some physical preparation, too. Clear the calendar (two weeks is ideal for a ten- to eleven-room home) as much as possible. Decide how much of your activities and responsibilities can be delegated, canceled, or postponed. If you're in a position where you never have unbroken, large blocks of time at home, still clear the calendar as much as you can and do the job a little at a time. Whatever your at-home schedule is like, you'll appreciate a simplified schedule during this project, so take deliberate steps to control the demands on your time until you've finished.
Plan menus ahead; include some Crock-Pot suppers and

freezer dishes. Also think about ordering dinner in, especially on the day or days you do the kitchen. Or treat your family to a meal at the nearest fast-food place.

● On the day of "overload attack," put your family on "alert." This is courteous and helps ensure their cooperation and involvement. And since they are most likely part of the problem, you'll need them to be part of the solution. Because streamlining involves much change, use all the psychology you can to ease them into it. (It's been said the only person who likes a change is a wet baby.) Reassure them that nothing will be tossed out that is needed, used, or dearly loved. You might want to discuss the quality versus quantity idea, and your desire to raise the entire family's standard of living. In the case of small children, you may want to inspect their rooms each morning before they go off to school or play, to encourage consistency with the new habits.

Let them know that they can depend on you to provide meals and clean laundry during the streamlining, but little else. Let them see and feel your positive attitude, enthusiasm, and seriousness over this project and your desire for improvement. And finally, state your faith in their ability to change and your appreciation of their promised cooperation.

● Gathering necessary supplies will be your last bit of preparation. These supplies will cost you little or no money. You'll probably be able to use what you already have. Here's what you need:

√Assorted containers for storage, give-away, and throw-away items.

√A dark marking pen for labeling boxes, bags, and cupboard containers.

√A permanent laundry marker for marking all children's play clothes labels.

√Yarn for tying up the charity bags. (The bags with twist-ties will have a different category of contents than the bags tied with yarn.)

√A small box with index cards in it for recording contents

BOX 21 — under stairs
1 - two sets popsicle makers
2 - Soccer uniform (size 6)
3 - two girls swimsuits blue (size 10)
4 - girls shorts (size 6-14)
5 - boys swimsuits (red size 8 blue size 10)
6 - b___ ___ts (size 4-12)
7 - ___e's swim towels

___X 6 — garage
1 - Christmas twinkle lights
2 - Christmas yard lights
3 - tree stand
4 - one bottle tree preserver
5 - tree skirt
6 - Christmas stockings

Storage at your fingertips is a benefit of using the card-file system.

and locations of all storage boxes. For instance, your keeper Christmas decorations will be put in a numbered container. On an index card with a corresponding number, you'll list each item in the box, then indicate its storage location. (See illustration.)

The benefits of this system are many: You hunt through only a card file for your item, rather than the entire house, thus saving time, energy, and wear and tear on nerves. You also have at your fingertips an accurate, ready inventory of all stored belongings. Thus, if you're considering purchasing a new Sunday dress for Susie, you can check your card file to see if you already have a dress her size, in good condition. (Remember, for anything to be a keeper and worthy of saving and storing, it must be in good condition.) Under this system, your storage areas work for, rather than against, you. No longer is there the possibility of storage areas becoming "lands of no return."

√ Paper and pencil for listing items that need to be purchased later. (Each room usually needs a few new things to help it meet its potential.) If you carry a want list on you when shopping, you're less apt to forget what you need.

KAREN'S ROOM

wants:	needs:
① new stenciling	① new lamp shade
② new bed- spread	② carpet cleaned
③ matching curtains	③ dresser handle
④ shelf	④ bulletin board
	⑤ framed mirror

You should have one "Wants and Needs List" for each room you are streamlining.

5

Mastering
the Master Bedroom

The master bedroom should be the most special room in your house. It's an adult retreat, the place above all the other rooms where peace and serenity can reign. It's your sanctuary, and it deserves to look the part. More important, you deserve this kind of bedroom.

Because you begin and end each day there, it has more of an influence on you than any other place in your home. Self-esteem starts here, first thing in the morning, every morning. Knowing that you have this room under control will make a big difference in how each day starts.

Despite its importance, the master bedroom in many homes doesn't get the attention—or affection—it deserves. Often, it's the last room to be decorated. Sometimes, it's the unofficial storage bin for the whole house. Clean laundry, unsorted and unfolded, covers the bed; magazines cover the floor; tennis racquets hide in the closet; general clutter and disarray are the order of the day.

Even if things are not quite so bad at your house, there are several good reasons to start your overhaul with the master bedroom.

• You'll need an orderly, under-control place to retreat to when you work on the rest of the house.

• A successfully simplified master bedroom will serve as a motivator and energizer while the rest of the house is deep in clutter.

• This room very likely holds a large percentage of sentimental things. That may make for some psychological barriers to the cleanup process, but once you've surmounted them here, you'll be well prepared to deal with the rest of the house. Doing the master bedroom first is like going through basic training—it's tough, but it prepares you for anything that follows.
What's more, after your dresser and closet are simplified, you'll no longer be wearing out-of-style clothes, too-tight clothes, too-big clothes, or otherwise unflattering clothes. (An added plus—you'll probably find that others show you greater courtesy, respect, and attention when your dress

consistently reflects self-respect and pride.) And delving into a dresser drawer where socks are tucked neatly inside themselves and nested by color in containers, and where only stockings in perfect condition are to be found, just makes you feel good.

Cleaning a simplified bedroom gives you a sense of control and accomplishment, too. In a simplified bedroom, you can vacuum the closet floor and even under the bed (now that's homemaking supreme!).

Now that you're convinced, here's what to do.

CLOSET

In any room that has one, the closet is the place to start. Use the key questions listed in Chapter 3 on every little thing in there. Start with the clothes rod. Don't worry about getting rid of too many clothes. Keep your standards high: quality over quantity is the watchword. Get rid of that load of unworn, sad-looking clothing and you'll enjoy the new items more. (Did you know that the average person wears 20 percent of his or her wardrobe 80 percent of the time? As you scrutinize your collection, you'll probably realize this is true for you.) Your favorite pieces are out front, within easy reach. The things you never wear are pushed far to the back.

You might want to have a friend help you with your clothing decisions. An outsider's objectivity could speed the job along. Take out only one thing at a time, and don't keep anything you think you'll make over. Chances are, your unfinished projects list is long enough right now, so you don't need to add anything more to it. (Old denims are legitimate keepers, however; the versatile fabric has so many more lives than just jeans—bat and ball drawstring bags, hats, even picnic quilts, for example.)

Establish a keeper pile of clothes as you fill the charity and garbage bags. Your keeper pile should be much smaller than the charity and garbage piles. When you rehang the keepers, group like items together for both an orderly look and greater efficiency.

Don't overlook the usefulness of inside closet walls. They're good places to hang purses, belts, ties, a lint brush, and so on. You'll find you don't need anything elaborate for this hanging business—finish nails and screw-in hooks work well.

Work on the closet shelf next. There's something about a shelf that seems to shout, "Things, things! Give me your poor, your tired, your wayfaring things!" But don't listen. Your shelf will do just fine and you'll like it better if you clear everything off except your memory box and possibly an extra blanket.

Now go to the floor and deal with the shoes. Whether you put your keepers on a rack, in boxes, in a bag, or just set them on the floor makes no difference. Just make sure you keep only quality and avoid duplicates (do you really need three pairs of sport shoes?). Don't give valuable space to dead shoes.

Shoes stop looking "right" once they reach a certain age. To insure a fresh, stylish look, buy high-quality shoes to start with; pay particular attention to the toe look and to the heel height and heel thickness; note the visual weight of the shoe sole; try to avoid flashy, faddish looks.

Footwear experts say shoe styles usually have a two-year to three-year life cycle. The first year a style emerges is considered the fast side. The third year in the life of this style is considered the slow side. Buying on the fast side enables you to get your money's worth out of your shoes; you'll look stylish longer, and therefore you'll want to wear the shoes longer.

When you're deciding how many pairs of shoes you need, remember what professional wardrobe planners say. They suggest you plan your wardrobe around two basic, harmonizing colors, then choose two or three pairs of shoes to match your wardrobe color choices. It's not necessary to have a rainbow-colored fleet of shoes.

Handle your partner's side of the closet like yours. Many are threatened by this at first, but most eventually come around. We're always asked what to do about resisters, and the best answer we can give is to consistently set a good example by keeping your own areas of responsibility

Boots hung from a skirt hanger will stay upright, not floppy.

For better boot storage, clip each pair at the top to a skirt hanger and hang, either from the clothes rod or on the back closet wall, below the skirt level, from a nail or hook. This takes care of the boot flops. (Be sure to wipe the heels and soles before hanging, to prevent dirt rubbing against walls or clothes.)

simplified and orderly; then be patient.

When the closet is finished, continue working in a clockwise pattern around the room, taking your four big containers with you. Deal with the next item or area you come to.

DRESSER

Let's say the next item is the dresser. Try to narrow down its function in your mind before you do anything else. This will help you empty and refill it properly. If you've decided it is to be used for certain categories of clothing, then out go the medicines and cosmetics, the hidden candy bars, the tube of tub-and-tile caulking, the orphaned keys, the memento-box things, and everything else that landed there because you didn't know where else to put it.

Work with the dresser as you did the closet, touching and considering one thing at a time. (You may have the impression as you read that this is a laboriously slow proc-

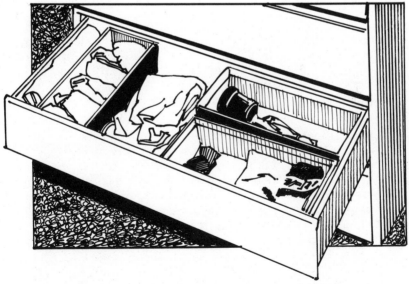

Using containers inside a dresser drawer gives permanent order and control.

ess. It is. But only for the first little bit, while you're in the closet. After you have worked like this for a while, you get the knack, you see the end result in your mind, and you pick up steam.)

Don't keep old, yellowed slips, or stretched-out bras (and don't save the hardware; you aren't going to reuse those hooks, and you know it). Get rid of all torn nylon stockings and socks. Toss out yellowed, tired jock straps.

Speaking of nylons, here's how to keep those delicate accessories protected and in control: hold the pantyhose at the waistband; fold the pantyhose in half, lengthwise, placing one leg next to the other; while still holding the pantyhose at the top with one hand, bring the toes of the stockings up to the waistband, with the other hand; bring the knees up to the waistband; continue folding the nylons up to the waistband until you have a small bundle, three to four inches long. Finally, fold the outside, sturdier tummy panel over the leg bundle, just as you fold a pair of crew socks together, by inserting your thumbs inside the outer layer, folding it down over the leg parts.

Here are some useful dresser tips:

- Use small containers, such as shoeboxes, inside the drawers to hold groups of things: bras, rolled-up nylons, scarves, belts (if you don't hang them in the closet), crew socks, pocket things, and so on.

- If you share a dresser, assign the top drawer to your partner. Put a small box inside to hold his pocket things.

- Fold full-slips in half by letting the top fall over the bottom as you hold it at the waist; then fold this in thirds lengthwise. Finish by folding it down, again in thirds. Lay slips in drawer flat, with lace edge showing. This technique works for half-slips and panties, too.

- Fold two-piece items, such as pajamas, by folding the bottoms over the folded top (this is a consolidation idea).

- Keep the dresser top clear except for one or two attractive items, such as a small plant, nicely framed photo, or dresser lamp. This will look nicer, expand your space visually, make dusting easy.

- Don't leave the dresser until you have made definite assignments to each drawer, it looks nice, and you're happy with

A dresser top with no more than two items makes for attractiveness, visual space, and easy dusting.

it. Change things around and experiment until your new system works for you.

UNDER THE BED

Dig it out, then keep it empty. There will be enough room throughout your home to accommodate all keepers from under your bed. So leave this space clear; it's easier to clean and it's a constant signal that you are in control. We've streamlined the smallest of homes, even single-width mobile homes, and we've always found better storage in other areas of the home. Try doing without under-bed storage for twenty-one days. If you're still not convinced, go back to storing under there, but at least do yourself the favor of grouping like items together and making specific assignments to this underneath area. There is one valid exception to this "no under-bed storage," however. This is the platform and waterbed with built-in storage

45

drawers. Deal with this type of storage as you do your dresser drawers.

NIGHT STANDS AND BEDSIDE TABLES

If you are sure you absolutely need one or two of these, then deal with them ruthlessly; they can be real clutter boxes. Maybe your nightstand's purpose is to hold a lamp, hold a clock radio or alarm clock, hold the phone, or hold all three. If there is a drawer or shelf, maybe this could hold the phone book, diary, or daily planning book. But basically, it ought to be clear and kept that way, for the same reasons as the dresser top.

WALLS

Even though we all deserve high-quality furnishings in our homes, what we deserve and what we have can be two different things. So while we are setting goals and making plans to get what we really want, let's use what we do have with taste and flair.

Walls are great places to add some style to a room. If your bedroom walls are plastered with eight years' and four kids' worth of grade-school-made Mother's Day and Christmas presents, then assign the most treasured to your memento box, hang the latest arrival(s) on your laundry area wall (this soothes the feelings of the gift givers and brightens a usually drab spot), and throw the less meaningful away. You might even take a picture of the child with the gift he gave you, then discard the item itself.

As you're deciding what to do with your walls, remember to watch out for the trendy look; hooped pictures may be cute, popular, easy-to-do, and inexpensive. But do they say anything specific about *you*? After all, this special room should radiate your personality, not that of the local craft class leader. Your own tastes, heritage, and background are a rich resource for decorative ideas; use these as inspiration for design statements about you. Be care-

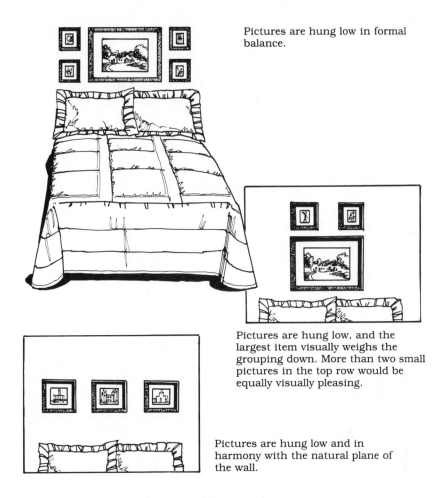

Pictures are hung low in formal balance.

Pictures are hung low, and the largest item visually weighs the grouping down. More than two small pictures in the top row would be equally visually pleasing.

Pictures are hung low and in harmony with the natural plane of the wall.

Examples of Good Picture Placement

ful, too, of visual clutter. Too much of anything is just that—too much. It's not tasteful or enhancing. Don't let empty wall space intimidate you. Interior designers work it into the decor because of its restful effects. So do your best to keep your walls elegant and *simple.*

Pay close attention to the balance and scale of the things you hang. Don't hang a tiny object all alone on a large wall; it will get lost and lose its effectiveness. Group it with some other things for greater impact. Don't hang a huge piece on a small wall, either. It's a good idea to visually divide your wall into vertical thirds and place objects along one of these invisible dividing lines. Avoid the tendency to place things in the exact center of any wall. The empty space on either of the "thirds" sides will balance the objects hung on the other side. When you hang things, try to keep a dominant single item, or the focal point of a group, at or below eye level.

Avoid hanging anything on service walls. (Service walls are those little slivers of wall that are found between door jambs and corners, or door jambs and other door—or window—jambs.) These four- to six-inch pieces of wall are meant for holding up door frames, not for decorating. They tend to look cluttered very quickly once you start using them as backgrounds for hanging objects.

CEDAR CHESTS AND OTHER EXTRAS

Sometimes a cedar chest is a place for extra bedding, sometimes a place for mementos. Whatever it holds, deal with each and every item inside it. Keep only positive things. Then, once it's loaded with keepers, deal with the chest itself. If it isn't attractive in its own right, maybe it could go into a behind-the-scenes storage area. After all, everything in your master bedroom should reflect your taste and style. If there is an item that doesn't do that, think about removing it.

Watch the general furniture overload in the master bedroom, too. You can visually open a room up by removing some furniture pieces. Don't let your bedroom be a dumping ground for extra furniture that you don't know what to do with. For example, Alice removed an office desk, her sewing machine cabinet, an old cedar chest, and a chair from her average-sized master bedroom. All this overload had shrunk the bedroom down to nothing. But she found other places for all the items, and the room looks twice as big now—and much better. If your room is small, you might consider putting your dresser, chest of drawers, or cedar chest in your closet.

Braving the Bath

Nobody loves a bathroom—but nobody wants to do without one, either. In fact, more than one—the higher the ratio of baths per person in your household, the better. But even having enough bathrooms to go around doesn't always mean any or all of them will be in the condition you'd like them to be.

Everyone knows that a bathroom is designed with hygiene, grooming, and sanitation in mind. It is important to remember, however, what a bathroom is *not*, because the more cluttered a bath is, the less efficiently it will perform its designated tasks. It is *not* a storage room, a library annex, a beauty supply or pharmaceutical warehouse. It *is* usually a small room with a minimum of space for anything other than the bare (!) essentials. It doesn't usually even lend itself to housing backup supplies of toilet paper and so on. So start simplifying each bath in your house by searching it for storage overload.

The basic purpose of this room is grooming and hygiene. The more cluttered the room is, the less effective it is for these tasks. As you evaluate the drawers, cupboards, and space under the sink, you'll probably find many unrelated things stored (or shoved) here and there. Curling irons, hair dryers, and hair grooming accessories such as combs, ribbons, rubber bands, and bobby pins are stuffed into drawers or shelves that you must dig through each time you need something. Or a bathroom drawer is so overloaded that hairbrushes roll in the stray squirts of toothpaste, and toothbrushes gather lost strands of hairbrush hair. And wallowing among all this may be orphaned puzzle pieces or lonely pennies. We've seen cupboards and under-sink areas stuffed with towels, bed linens, and unrelated miscellany. We've found the toilet plunger, loads of cleaning supplies, and a toilet brush buried under a pile of dirty laundry.

Survey the countertops, back of the toilet tank, window sills, and corners of the tub. More than likely you'll see the makings of a small drugstore, with an inventory of hairspray and deodorant cans, shampoo, bubble bath, perfume bottles—even plants. Weed out some of this stuff so the maintenance will be easier and the space will visually expand. You'll find better places to store your daily grooming products—the shampoo and creme rinse, the shaving cream and razor, the bath powder and lotion, and so on. Your overall goal will be to put these things closest to their point of use. Your bedroom closet shelf, a dresser drawer, and a hall closet shelf are a few possibilities if you have no bathroom vanity or other bathroom storage. Work to keep your surfaces clear and you can keep them clean.

THE VANITY

Any vanity, regardless of size, serves you better if its contents are assigned to specific spaces. This will stop things from drifting and scattering.

Drawers: If your vanity has drawers, you're lucky. Some drawers will need smaller containers put in them for grouping small similar items together. A drawer assigned to hair accessories will be fun to get into when all barrettes, rubber bands, combs, clips, and so on are in their own containers. If you need to make more than one assignment per drawer, be sure you group like items together in small containers.

Under the sink: Lots of possibilities here. First, double your space by installing a shelf in the back, under the pipes. Second, insert hooks into the underside of the vanity top. Third, insert hooks or finish nails into the inside vanity walls and on the inside of vanity doors. What's being stored under the sink determines how far apart your hooks and nails are. Careful, though, don't overload. This space works best if it is efficient but not too full.

The shelf in the back is a good place for an extra pack of toilet paper, a cleaning bucket, or the plunger. Whatever you put on the back shelf, remember that it's somewhat hard to reach, so don't assign things to it that you need three or four times a day, such as a container of combs and brushes. Incidentally, there's nothing sacred about the

A shelf and finish nails multiply under-the-sink storage space in a vanity.

length of a plunger handle. If yours has a long handle, saw four or five inches off; then it will fit nicely under any sink.

From the nails and hooks you inserted, you could hang the curling iron, blow dryer, and drawstring bags. Drawstring bags are among the neatest things around— they efficiently utilize ignored and wasted space. Use them to hold curlers, feminine hygiene needs, hair clippers plus attachments, a few bars of soap, even your makeup if there is no other place. You will think of a dozen more drawstring-bag ideas. (You may want to label the bags— or make them out of different fabrics—so you can easily tell what's inside them.)

The vanity floor could hold a wicker basket or a large juice or shortening can of brushes and combs. You might also want a cleaning bucket sitting here, holding a spray bottle of hospital disinfectant, a cleaning cloth, and a plastic scrubber. Try to keep the floor as clear as possible, though, to make it easy to keep clean. (See illustration.)

Vanity top: Keep it as clear as possible. Keeping the top clear will open up the room and expand your space, visually. And a clear top is much easier to clean.

SHELVES, CUPBOARD, CLOSET, MEDICINE CABINET

You want these storage areas to be efficient rather than full. Storing all keepers in labeled containers will encourage efficiency. Toothbrushes do not need to sit in a holder on the vanity top. After all, you will pay a maintenance price for that holder. Consider putting the holder under the sink, inside a cupboard or medicine chest, or group the brushes into a tray-type drawer organizer.

If you're interested in eliminating some laundry loads and buying some space, don't stock these areas with linens. Instead, practice our "No-Linen Closetology." Assign each bathroom a certain towel color and each family member his or her own towel and wash cloth. You might add lace, eyelet, or monograms for easier identification. Put one extra set in the cupboard or drawer for emergencies, and box up the best of the rest to go into storage. If you have any "on the way out" towels, pair them up with all the swimsuits in the family. With a laundry marker, label each swim towel, then box up these suit-towel combinations for storage, too.

Now you have good family towels and wash cloths hanging on your towel racks, each to be used over again by their respective owners until you launder them. Then they're taken off the rack, laundered, and put back on the rack the same day.

These towels may wear out a little sooner, but we believe the space this system buys and the potential lighter laundry load are well worth it.

NO STORAGE
(NO VANITY, NO SHELVES, NO . . .)

We've lived with this and it's tough, but not impossible. Living the Law of Household Physics helps. Minimum spaces suggest the need for minimum stuff. So the first step in coping with a storageless bathroom is to get down to absolute essentials as if your sanity depended on it.

If you have a partner's shaving and grooming gear to worry about, deal with that first. Assuming there's at least a medicine cabinet in your bathroom, store that gear in it. Then come the grooming aids—toothbrushes, toothpaste, deodorant. A typical medicine chest won't hold much more, so your makeup, in a container, will go someplace else—a corner of one of your dresser drawers, part of your closet shelf, in a drawstring bag hanging on your closet wall. Consider keeping your good set of tweezers in an unidentified, only-you-know-where place, away from the set your children use.

All remaining bathroom inventory will also go someplace else. No more hiding the cracked tile and the mold growing along the tub ledge with the bubble bath, shampoo, and conditioner. If there's a shower head, a shower caddy is a legitimate need and will keep some of the items out of the way. No more using the window sill and back of the toilet tank as makeshift shelves. Get rid of the visual clutter and the maintenance drudgery by putting your keepers someplace else, such as a closet shelf or cupboard in either the master bedroom or hall closet; use a set of hanging wire baskets, or a small wicker trunk under the sink if there's room.

DIRTY LAUNDRY

Does your bathroom resemble the aftermath of a hurricane, with dirty clothes and towels strewn all over? Misplaced laundry creates tremendous irritation and inconvenience. To improve this situation, make a specific place for dirty laundry. When there's a designated spot for dirty laundry, the responsibility for keeping it picked up rests flat on family shoulders.

If you use a laundry hamper, consider giving it up. They are space eaters, and most bathrooms have little space to sacrifice. They must constantly be moved for floor sweeping and mopping. They get smelly, and even the most expensive can look tacky after awhile.

If you don't have a slick system for laundry, try this: Buy or sew a hanging closet laundry bag for each person in your household. This solution is inexpensive and takes little space. The bag can be washed as needed.

BATH TOYS

When it comes to children, what's a bath without toys? But don't get carried away: allow only certain toys to be played with in the tub. And provide a drip-dry storage container, such as a nylon or plastic mesh bag, that the bather can hang up when he's through with the toys.

THE BATHROOM VERSUS TEENS

Teenagers need it as simple as a four year old—but this need is complicated by the fact that they have and use much more bathroom paraphernalia than a four year old. They can handle tossing the blow dryer into a drawstring bag, but they seldom cope with winding and securing the cord. So if you want your teen to help maintain bathroom order without weeping and wailing and gnashing of teeth, keep it simple.

BATHROOM SCALES

One of life's recurring minor annoyances is tripping over the bathroom scales. To avoid this, stand them up against a wall, put them under the sink, or hang them on the inside of a cabinet wall.

FIRST AID SUPPLIES

A few minor emergency supplies, such as Band-Aids, petroleum jelly, tweezers, rubbing alcohol, hydrogen peroxide, and so on, can be stored in the bathroom if you have a secure place. Keep the larger, more extensive kit in a high cupboard, above the refrigerator, or on a high shelf in the hall closet. Discard old medicines; store the keepers where they are taken, and out of reach of children. Group like items together in a labeled container.

GUEST BATH

If you are fortunate enough to have a guest bath, or even if you just want to welcome an occasional guest, here's a nice idea. Group a good set of towels, new toothbrushes, toothpaste, disposable razor, soaps, and shampoo together in a drawstring bag or pretty basket. Bring this out when company arrives—you'll feel like a gracious hostess and they will appreciate the convenience.

7

Starting Fresh:
The Baby's Room

For a baby's room to be a baby's room, the approach is basic: Get everything that isn't baby-related out. As clothes are outgrown, move them out; for safety as well as neatness, don't store older children's toys in the baby's room.

CLOSET AND DRESSER

Babies need only a few pieces of dress-up clothing, and even these items rarely require closet space. So you can count on closet room to store things such as the playpen, walker, stroller, infant seat, even the diaper pail. Hang as much as you can, rather than stacking these things on top of each other on the floor. The closet shelf can hold one or two extra blankets or quilts, and the baby's memento box, with the baby book in it.

With a baby comes a diaper bag. This is like the family car keys or mother's purse . . . it is easy to misplace if it hasn't been assigned a specific resting place. A suggestion: Hang the bag on a wooden hanger in baby's closet, or on a sturdy hook in the closet wall.

If the closet seems like the best place for diaper storage, a hanging diaper organizer or stacker will help you. (You'd be surprised at how often we have seen clean diapers wadded up in a laundry basket in some remote corner of a baby's room. Plowing through laundry baskets is a time-and-energy waster, not to mention what it does to the room's appearance.) If you use disposables, get them out of the bulky box and put them in a diaper organizer.

Be ruthlessly realistic as you streamline baby clothes. Typically, sentimentality and frugality make it difficult to get rid of very much here, but don't give in to these forces. Toss out stained and worn clothes. Put clothing that doesn't currently fit, into a labeled box and into the storage area (see Chapter 17). Special pieces, such as a christening outfit, the cap and booties Grandma crocheted, a first pair of shoes, and so on, deserve a place in a child's memento box. Fold play outfits as separate units, top inside the matching bottom, and place them in a drawer; hang up dressy clothes. But remember: You will buy space and save on laundry time if you keep out only a minimum number of clothes.

Put containers in the dresser drawers for control. If there's space, put undershirts in one container, socks and booties in another container, plastic pants in another, all in one drawer. Put pajamas there, too, if you have room. Play shirts, pants, and rompers could go in another drawer, and sweaters and outer clothing still another. Any extra drawer space could be devoted to diaper storage if you prefer this to the closet diaper stacker.

OTHER FURNITURE

It's nice to have a rocking chair and changing table in a baby's room if there is space. But if you don't have enough space for the rocker, dresser, changing table, plus the crib, then make some choices. If the dresser is a low one, it can double as a changing table; or the standard-size changing table can serve as a dresser. Another possibility: Put the dresser or chest of drawers inside the closet.

If baby hygiene takes place here, then put related supplies, such as powder, cream, lotion, cotton swabs, cotton balls, and so on in a container (those glorious shoeboxes . . .) inside a drawer for convenience. If there is no drawer space to accommodate these things, then perhaps they could sit on the closet shelf and be taken down as needed. We suggest you store nothing under the crib; you'll thank us when you're vacuuming.

To unclutter the room visually, get everything off those window sills. Remember, too, that your dusting and window washing will go much faster if you don't have to move the powder, oil, and so on.

TOYS

An infant becomes a baby, a baby becomes a toddler, and on it goes. But a rattle stays a rattle, long after the baby loses interest in it. So keep pace with baby's stages of growth and development—and keep his toys rotated accordingly. Clear out anything baby is not currently using.

WHAT ABOUT SHARED ROOMS?

Babies' rooms are often small, if you're lucky enough to even *have* this room. So the most important point is: keep it simple and easy to maintain. But how do you do this if baby must share his space with the sewing machine, an office desk, or even other people? Although the introduction to this chapter advised getting everything that isn't baby-related out, we recognize that in this space-crunched world, baby doesn't always have a private room. If that's the case at your house, divide the room up and make specific assignments to each area. Keep everything in the room in containers and allow only a bare minimum in there. Hang as much as possible.

Roommates manage their spaces better if Mother removes ownership ambiguity as much as possible—"This is Bill's shelf, this is Brian's shelf; this is Bill's drawer, this is Brian's drawer . . .," and so on. Spaces may need labeling to aid the memory.

GOING SOLO

What about the lucky child whose room is *his* throughout his stay-at-home years? Keep it simplified throughout those years. The furnishings and decor should keep pace with the child's stages of growth and development. So don't store nonused clothes, toys and games, furniture, accessories, and so on in this room. Assuming they are still keepers, move them to an appropriate storage area (see Chapter 17). When we start storing things in prime living spaces (bedrooms, bathrooms, and so on) they can take on a warehouse appearance. We all know warehouses are not comfortable or attractive. No one enjoys sharing living space with storage, and few of us can do this efficiently—children rarely can.

DECORATING DEVICES

How do you keep a baby's room simple yet stimulating? Try thoughtful application of bright colors, cheerful curtains, maybe a mobile above the crib, and some good wall decor in bright colors and simple shapes. Stenciling can do wonders. For example, Alice decorated an entire nursery wall with simple coloring book pictures. If you'd like to try this, section the wall off with painted lines, using masking tape as a straight-edge guide. Then with pencil draw a picture in each box. Finish it off by painting each picture with bright acrylics.

While many vinyl wall coverings are bright and washable, the beauty of stenciled or painted decorating is its affordability and flexibility. As the child outgrows the decor, it can be painted over and some other design applied.

You can repeat the theme by using the same technique on solid-colored, inexpensive fabric, to be made into curtains. Section off the fabric using straight lines, then draw a picture in each space, using fabric crayons.

8

Keep Up the Good Work: Creating a Kid-Ready Room

In this chapter we'll discuss both the young child's room and the teenager's room. They both suffer from basically the same problems and are both dealt with in basically the same way, but there are two differences—the age and interest level of the things involved, and who does the simplifying. *You* do the child's room; you *train* the teen to do his own room.

Maybe over the years of struggling with the chronic messy world of youth, you thought it might be easier to just shut the door, make the best of the mess, and hope time would cure the problem (maturity, it's called). Don't give in to those feelings, and don't give up the struggle.

Your children need order; they flourish and thrive in it. Asking a child to clean up a perpetually overloaded room is not reasonable—he can't cope with overload any better than you can (actually he does much worse, because immaturity works against him). But he tries, shoving, cramming, hiding things here and there, hoping this time you won't notice what he's really done. You do notice, you are on his back, and he's in the doghouse. It's an eternal cycle, with no positive results in sight. But ask a child to clean up a simplified room, and you've found a reasonable task that's within his abilities. He deals with the minimum mess properly, you are pleased, and he's happy. So break the negative cycle and lay the groundwork for a positive cycle to begin.

Sometimes the origin of the overload isn't your immediate family, of course. There are many sources, and one of the hardest to deal with is extended family and well-meaning friends. One favor you could do your children, as well as yourself, is to give your relatives and friends some suggestions for meaningful, long-lasting gifts—examples might include sports and college pennants, hair salon gift certificates, hope chest items, "special" bedding such as hand-tied quilts, "time-with-you" coupons, good books, or a clip-on headboard reading lamp.

Whatever the origins of the problem, your prime goal in streamlining a child's room is to create a world that a child can maintain mostly by himself. Overload causes him to avoid decision making when pickup time arrives; the less he has to deal with, the easier and quicker his decision making will be. You also want the child's standard of living to be high: His room should look (and smell) clean, be attractive and comfortable, and radiate positive messages. First of all, assess the overall condition of the room, and if it needs it, make plans for improvement. It doesn't take any longer to maintain nice things than it does to maintain shabby, worn-out, tacky things. Be sure to use your paper and pencil to record the "wants" and "needs" for this room.

It is helpful if *all* the child's or teen's belongings are gathered into his room so you can get a full picture of what you have to deal with. Retrieve his dirty laundry to make sure it's all in the keepers category, and so you can more efficiently plan space for storing it when it is clean. If toys, sports equipment, art materials, books, and so on are scattered throughout the house, retrieve them also, and allow space for them in the bedroom.

A word on preparing the teenager: Use psychology. If he is handled right, he'll want you to teach him how and he'll be anxious to do it. Don't press or nag; maybe even let his room wait while you do the rest of the house. He'll observe what is happening, see the results, and want the same thing for himself. You may need to bring in outside help. Sometimes one of your friends can be more effective with a teen than you yourself can. But above all, be pleasant, be patient, be persistent.

Now you're ready to begin your clockwise pattern. Make a sweep around the floor first. As before, evaluate each item you come to, using the key questions. What doesn't go in the charity, trash, someplace else, or to-file box is a keeper for the room. Just as you did in the master bedroom, establish a keeper pile, somewhere in the room, but out of the way. The things from this pile will "melt" into the room's empty spaces you create with your streamlining. After you have simplified the floor, begin working on the closet.

CLOTHES

After all the child's clothes are gathered, you'll probably have four categories of children's wear:

√Play clothes
√School clothes
√Dressy clothes
√Discards (those that go either to charity or the garbage)

Use these categories as you simplify. A child doesn't need lots of extra clothing to keep neat and tidy in his closet and dresser, and you don't need them in your laundry each week. A child's basic needs include eight pairs of socks and underwear (one on, one in the laundry, six in the drawer). If you wash at least once a week, then he only needs seven play outfits and maybe one dressy outfit.

Separate keeper clothing this way: underwear, socks, and play clothes go in the dresser; school and dressy clothes go in the closet. Place socks, underwear, and undershirts in smaller containers inside the drawer for control. This way, even if the child rummages through a container looking for that certain pair of underwear, it's only the underwear container that's a shambles, and not the entire drawer. Fold play outfits together (as we described for two-piece items in the master bedroom and baby's room chapters). Match up school outfits too, hanging a coordinated shirt over a pair of pants, and a coordinated blouse over a matching skirt. You can see how this system raises a child's standard of living. You've removed the chance for a child to look tacky or bedraggled.

School outfits will stay looking nicer longer (even if this is just jeans and sweatsuits) if the child changes into play clothes after school. (Play clothes are the patched or faded jeans, the sweatsuits with the patched knee; anything that's lost that "just bought" sparkle, yet has plenty of wear left.)

Everywhere we go, people ask what to do with their mountains of hand-me-downs. Here are our three rules:

- Keep only quality. Don't store play clothes—the child is in the process of creating his own. Look for a worn seat, underarms, elbows, and stains; look for lost shape, especially in knits, and look for faded fabric.
- Mend keepers before storing. This lessens the chance that they'll become dead storage and increases their chances of being used.

In this corner of a kid's room, college pennants hang at ceiling level to add interest as well as visual space; posters hang as a grouping, occupying floor-to-ceiling space; and a minimum is kept on the dresser top.

- Store efficiently. You can label one end of a box so the contents can be noted at a glance. But if you have a great variety and quantity of storage boxes, we suggest you take Daryl Hoole's advice. She says store in numbered boxes, and keep a 3x5 card on every box of stored items, matching the number of the card to the number of the box. Itemize box contents on the card and indicate the storage location. This will increase chances of these items being worn. Store only what can be used, then use what you store.

Living the Law of Household Ecology (when something new comes in, something else must go out) is one of the best things you can do to keep control of the number of clothes you manage. When you add new clothes, get rid of some old clothes. Sounds almost wasteful: after all, won't you need all those clothes some day? Probably not—but you will always need your space.

Keep an ever-filling charity bag or box in your laundry area. Clothes are always in a state of wearing out, being grown out of, going out of style. Don't give clothes a lifetime parking space in any dresser or closet.

Keep the dresser top clear also. A child can probably handle a lamp, a framed photo, or both. But remember, you're trying to create a room your child can maintain. Make it easy for him.

TOYS, BOOKS, GAMES, SPORTS EQUIPMENT

Streamline to weed out all the broken toys; tired stuffed animals; books with broken backs, lost covers, and ripped pages; and games with broken or missing pieces. Check the interest rating on these things, too. If they no longer hold interest, get rid of them.

Toys will pay for themselves and earn their keep if they are high-quality and open-ended or "doing" toys (such as blocks, dolls, toy dishes, building sets such as Lincoln Logs and interlocking plastic blocks, and so on). Toys that draw on the imagination are a child's friend for years.

Group toys into small drawstring bags or containers

A truck-shaped pegboard is an attractive decoration as well as a useful drawstring-bag holder.

with lids. These full drawstring bags can be hung on an inside closet wall or from a wall-mounted peg board, with pegboard hooks. Alice's children use large pegboards cut in shapes and decorated to match their room decor. For instance, her boys' room is trimmed in paneled truck stenciling, so their pegboard is cut in the shape of this paneled truck and painted to match. Her daughters' pegboard is cut in the shape of a house. (See illustrations.) Each shape is approximately 4 feet high and 5 feet long.

Be sure to rotate toys from time to time, putting some up out of sight. Keep a selection tucked away to bring out whenever a babysitter comes, too—this eases a potentially tense situation for everyone.

Doll collections can sit on a child's bed, in a cradle or buggy, in a child's rocker, or on a low shelf. Some types of dolls, such as the ever-popular Barbie dolls, can be kept in drawstring bags, with their clothing and accessories.

Books are a child's window on the world; they become warm friends forever. Make good books a part of your home. Preserve preschool and some choice children's books by folding strips of clear, wide library tape over the bottom edge of each page to keep page edges from tearing. (This tape can be purchased at most office-supply stores.) Three-inch-wide strips of clear contact paper can serve the same purpose. Special treasures such as scouting handbooks will live longer and become permanent records of advancement if you cover the outside completely with clear contact paper.

Don't give space to games no one likes, or games with broken or missing pieces. Keep only family favorites. Get the keepers out of their rickety cardboard boxes. (We're convinced cardboard game-boxes do more than their share to undermine the mental health of the American homemaker.) Keep the instructions, though, by gluing them on the backs of their respective game boards. Group all like game parts together into little containers, placing tokens in one container, marbles in another, dice in another, and so on. Store these small containers together in one large container.

Try to centralize all sports equipment. Group it together in like categories and store in one central location. We use a heavy drawstring bag for all balls, bats, and mitts. Drawstring bags give order and control to practically any category of sports equipment. And these bags can

Board games are more manageable when removed from their cardboard boxes and stored in containers.

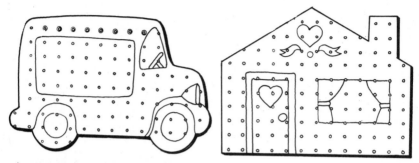

The pegboards in Alice's children's rooms are part of the decor—a truck for the boys, and a house for the girls.

be hung from studs along garage or storage area walls. Bagging things up isn't a guarantee that there will be no more roller skates or baseball bats lying in the middle of the front walk or on the basement stairs, but it's a help. And the system will at least free a child's closet and bedroom space of some clutter.

> For making drawstring bags, consider saving some "tosser" men's pants. Cut the legs off at the crotch. Turn inside out, sew straight across the bottom, and you have an automatic bag. Turn right side out and run your drawstring through the belt loops. (For more help and drawstring bag ideas, see Back-of-the-Book Bonuses.)

WALLS

Like the master bedroom, a child's or teen's room is not finished until you deal with the walls. Keep them simple, set standards, and exert some control over what will and will not be displayed in your children's rooms. See to it that your child's immediate world—his room—is a positive world. You might be able to talk your poster-loving child into rotating a few, as you do the toys, for a fresh and uncluttered look. Traditional wall items include a framed mirror, bulletin board, college or sports pennants, framed photos of the child and family, framed art prints, stenciling, and wall graphics.

Take time to teach the older children the same basic design principles discussed in the master bedroom chapter: talk about balance and scale of objects in relation to the wall, placement of objects on the wall, and so on.

MAKING THE IMPROVEMENT LAST

Keeping the room simplified means you will need to thoroughly orient your children as to what goes where and why it goes there. You'll also need to be consistent with the morning room inspection. This is the one action that will tell children you're serious about this change. From now on there will be no more overload mismanagement. This kid-ready room will be a constant source of opportunities for a reasonable amount of responsibility, and you'll see consistent, positive results.

9

The World's Window
on You:
The Living Room

A living room isn't as purely functional as a bath or kitchen; nor is it as personal as a bedroom. Yet it's a key room in almost every home—the room visitors see first, sometimes the only room they spend time in. For that reason, many homemakers take greater pains with this room than with any other room in the house to make it look just right.

When it comes to simplifying, you may find there is not as much obvious clutter here as elsewhere, precisely because the living room is so public a space. This isn't always the case, though—some living rooms are the center of their homes' traffic patterns, and look it, with all the scattered possessions that go with a central location. Sometimes living room clutter is more subtle—a classic case of surface neatness, or decorative items that don't represent your family's values, tastes, and interests. Whichever type of overload you're seeing in your living room, the cure should be a familiar one to you by now.

Before you start the actual simplifying process, determine the specific purpose or purposes of *your* living room. That's not as obvious as it sounds, since this differs from home to home, depending on what other rooms are available, the age (and number) of family members, and the lifestyle that prevails at your house. If, for example, you have another room for TV watching, then you can reserve the living room for conversation, entertaining, reading, and similar pursuits. One thing your living room should not be is a kitchen annex: we've seen living rooms where people regularly ate and drank, at the visible expense of the furnishings and carpet. Save your furnishings (and your cleanup time) by limiting food consumption to the kitchen or dining room.

Once the purpose is assigned, hold to it. Family or recreation rooms are better for active pastimes, if you have such rooms. The living room, ideally, is the place for best behavior, good manners, decorum. If there are children in your home, the living room can serve as the laboratory for practicing their social graces.

CLEARING CLUTTER

Getting rid of living room overload starts with getting rid of outdated newspapers (even if you haven't read them yet), magazines, and catalogs. Sort through and tear out articles that you'll want to file; put these in the "to file" box. Make this routine a habit in the future to avoid repeat newspaper/magazine buildup. Don't try to take care of your "to file" box until your entire home is streamlined. You'll find that after every space in your house is simplified and under control, you'll have not only the physical but the mental energy to tackle what can be a most overwhelming chore—the files. In fact, for many chronic clippings collectors who are often paralyzed at the thought of tackling this job, we sometimes advise junking past collections and starting afresh.

The living room piano is a classic site of potential clutter. Sheet music and music books are usually the biggest problem. If you have the old-fashioned—and very practical—type of piano bench with a seat that opens up for storage, be sure to use that space. Or put the most frequently used materials atop or beside the piano in a book-sized wicker or rattan basket or other attractive container with handles. This basket can stand alongside the piano, and when practice is over, the books are easy to put away in their assigned spot; when they're needed for lessons, it's easy to carry along the entire container. Separate music into different categories, according to difficulty level or type. Consider putting music that is rarely used somewhere farther from the piano—for example, on a shelf in a bookcase or built-in storage unit. If you have a lot of music stored this way, you might want to set up a filing system so you can find specific pieces easily.

Besides being smothered by piles of music, the piano top also has a tendency to collect family photographs, stacks of mail, knickknacks, children's school papers, and the proverbial trailing philodendron. To clear the surface, mount the photos attractively on the wall, assign another drop-off spot for mail and school papers, and ruthlessly evaluate the knickknacks with intentions to eliminate some. If there's no better place for the philodendron, try winding it back through itself for a more compact, fuller plant. Clearing the piano top will create a fresh appearance as well as make for easier dusting.

Living room walls and table surfaces are often magnets for clutter, too. Because walls and other flat surfaces can have so much visual impact in a room, they are often decorating statements, whether you've made them so consciously or unconsciously. Think about it. Are visitors getting the impression you own stock in the wicker industry? Are you filling your walls with trendy or faddish decor only because you don't know what else to put there? There's nothing wrong with any of the decorating ideas we've just mentioned, *if* you really like them, *if* you don't overdo them, and *if* they are meaningful to you. Even if it means having some bare spots on your walls, you'll find greater satisfaction if what is hung on the walls reflects your individuality, values, and family personality.

Evaluate window sills, fireplace mantels, and hearths. Knickknack and accessory overload can easily get the best of these spots. Collect things that have special meaning to you, because you will be sacrificing space to hold them, and time and energy to care for them. Avoid overloading these tempting areas with too many sentimental or trendy knickknacks. There is a place in our homes and lives for the sentimental, but not at the expense of function, order, and good taste. Be sure your accessories are saying what you want them to about you.

For example, one woman who attended one of our seminars asked us what to do with the many antique porcelain dolls that were resting all over her living room. In talking with her, we could tell they meant a great deal to her and she really didn't want to part with them. The solution: Get rid of every bit of clutter so that these treasures can be seen and get the attention they deserve. Then group them together, perhaps in pretty oak-splint baskets or antique chairs. That type of approach will work with many collections. The key is to make sure that what you want to be noticed *is* noticed.

UNCONDITIONAL SURRENDER

Get rid of all living room furnishings and accessories that have broken parts or are tattered and torn beyond repair. Constantly using and looking at shabby or shoddy items is depressing. One attractive lamp is much better than two or three that desperately need junking. Sometimes it's better to go without until you can have something of quality. After all, possessions are a subtle reflection of our attitudes and self-image.

Consider, too, the quantity of furnishings in relation to the size of the room. Is there too much stuff? If so, can some pieces be put to better use in other rooms? Here's another reason to evaluate motives. Are you trying to impress someone? Are *things* giving you your identity? Are the people living in the home as precious to you as all the stuff you're collecting? Are visitors picking up the right message about how you feel about self, family, values, interests, and so forth? Even if your furniture is in good repair and beautiful, too much of a good thing is overwhelming and visually confusing. Remove some of the pieces and see if the effect isn't calmer and more peaceful.

DECORATIVE DEVICES

True, we've just finished warning you about decorating for the sake of decorating. But here are some ideas you may not have come across that you may want to adapt for your own use.

• If you are fortunate enough to have a front entry hall, hanging a nicely framed or pleasingly shaped mirror on one of its walls is a charming and practical touch. A mirror placed here will be convenient for both you and your guests—a good place for you to check your "face value" before opening the door or for your guests to have a glance before entering a room full of people.

• Plants enhance any room if they're well maintained

78

and properly positioned. They're especially useful for adding a lived-in and furnished look to a sparsely furnished living room. For greater impact, and to avoid having "lived-in" turn to "cluttered," group plants together rather than scattering them one to a section. And, of course, display only healthy-looking plants in clean, attractive containers. If you hate discarding a plant that's starting to look tired, move it to a less-public room and try to nurse it back to health.

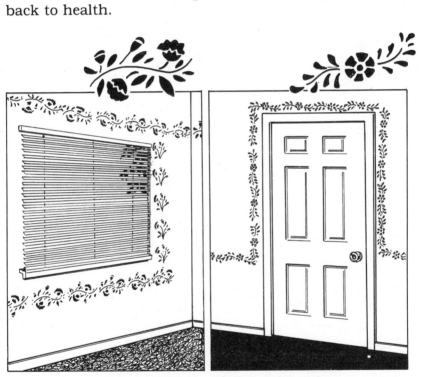

Stenciling can be applied around a living-room window or door.

● Stenciling is an inexpensive, attractive, and personal approach to living room decorating, just as it is for other rooms. (See Chapter 7 for more about it. We've also listed some helpful and appealing books on the subject under Suggested Reading on page 174.) Consider stenciling borders along the top of your walls to substitute for built-in moldings; you can create a similar effect at chair-rail level, or a dress-up effect around simply treated windows.

Items handed down from past generations form a unique and personal wall grouping.

● Another idea is to create a meaningful display of family heritage and ancestry items. Pauline's family room wall, for example, holds a few iron tools that her husband's father and grandfather used for years on their family farm. Alice's dining area wall holds a porcelain alphabet bowl that her husband's father used for meals when he was a small child. The same wall holds a quilted hanging made from an ancient General Mills flour sack, with logo and printing intact. Her mother and grandmother saved these cloth sacks, tried to bleach them white, and made them over into slips, panties, pantaloons, and dish towels. Your family crest or some handiwork from your ancestors' native land (or lands) is an effective way to establish a family legacy. It's also a refreshing change and can do a lot to make your home uniquely yours.

PROBLEM SOLVING: WORDS AND PICTURES

Not all living rooms (and the families who live in them) have the luxury of being fully furnished, beautifully pro-

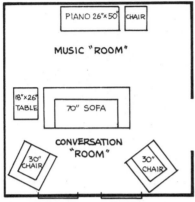

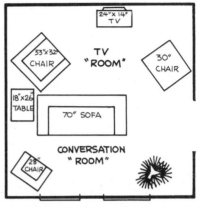

Centered sofa, room-within-a-room.   Back-to-back, room-within-a-room.

Living room 13'x13'9"

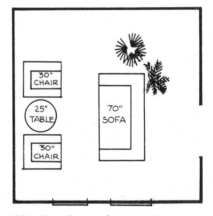

Minimum of furniture; plants fill   "Shrinking" space by arranging a
in spaces.   room around an imaginary wall.

portioned, or used just for quiet adult activities. If you live
in a rental unit, you may not even be able to experiment
much, if at all, with stenciling, other paint treatments, or
wall hangings without risking financial penalties. But no
matter what your dwelling, you *can* make your living room
a place you're proud to welcome guests to. Remember, it's

Pictures placed low on a wall fill space when furniture is sparse.

not what you have, but what you do with what you have
that counts.

So experiment until you like what you have. You
might, for example, group your furniture in arrangements
to give the appearance of a room-within-a-room—especially effective if you have only a few pieces to fill up a gener-
ous-sized space. Try placing a large piece, such as a sofa,
in the approximate center of the room. Or use a back-to-

82

back grouping. A combination of both techniques also works well to achieve a room-within-a-room look. The basic idea is to stop lining the walls with furniture. You might also try to create new "walls" in your imagination, and place all or the majority of your living room furniture in one part of the room.

Another budget-wise technique you can use to "furnish" a streamlined, sparsely furnished room is to place your wall decor low. This treatment visually takes the place of furniture and makes a room feel full because you are filling in spaces. Because attention naturally gravitates to walls, the room will look and feel more completely furnished if the walls are done well.

10

The Room
You REALLY Live In

Somewhere in your house, there's probably a room where everyone congregates; you may call it the den, or the family room, or the rec room, but whatever its name, it serves the same purpose. If you're fortunate enough to have such a room, you've probably noticed that it has a tendency to be a "nobody cares" room. "Don't eat that popcorn in the living room—take it to the family room," or "You can play with your toys in the family room," or "If you're going to wrestle, do it in the family room" are common instructions in many a household. This room, by any name, is a carefree, casual place because it's often out of sight of the living room, and therefore of the outside world. It gets messy, cluttered, even abused. All the same, there's much more to it than that. In fact, a nicer way to think of this all-purpose place is the "make-yourself-at-home room."

An activity center is created when all board games are stored together.

Well, if you're going to have a place that's comfortable but also well maintained and uncluttered, you'll need to take a good look around the family room and figure out where comfort ends and shabbiness or carelessness begins. Take a look at the worn-out sofa, worn-through or stained carpet, broken-backed books, drooping draperies, flat cushions, and so on. Then think how carefully you've decorated your living room, putting your best effort out front. Don't subject yourself and your family—who deserve the best—to leftovers. Don't relegate unfixables, or things you've never liked, to the family room; don't be afraid to discard items that aren't good enough. Turn this room into one that can be care-free, but never care-less.

Start by deciding on a purpose or purposes for the room. It may be the place in your home with the most diverse assignments, so carefully define each area of the room and insist that your decisions be honored. This is an excellent place to use a room-within-a-room furniture arrangement. (See Chapter 9.) You can direct your attention into specific areas by creating activity centers inside this single family room space.

A room-within-a-room arrangement provides seating near the television and frees the rest of the room for other activity centers.

Encourage hobbyists to work in a family-room hobby center by storing all supplies there.

For example, if your family room houses a television, group comfortable seating around it, leaving space for other activities in the remainder of the room. If the negative influences of television concern you, look for ways to play down its attraction as much as possible. A dark empty screen begs to be turned on, so try turning it around, put it in a closet when it's not in use, or (here's our best and boldest suggestion) get rid of it.

You'll find the remainder of the space in the family room has lots of possibilities. Consider creating a hobby center with a table and chairs (small ones for the children). Or use floor cushions or beanbag chairs grouped around bookshelves to create a reading corner; place an area rug close to toy containers to make an inviting play center. If your family room includes a Ping-Pong or pool table, then keep everything that relates to it in one area, and all related pieces in one container. Your family may have totally different interests—but you get the idea. No matter how your family spends its time, you can develop attractive centers that will catch their attention and make them welcome in the special room of your home.

GETTING RID OF BOOKS:
IT'S A DIRTY JOB,
BUT SOMEONE HAS TO DO IT

Your family room may double as a family library. And that's great—books have a magic about them and are a wonderful part of any life and any home. But that very magic sometimes makes it hard to get rid of them. Since even books carry with them a space and maintenance price, they, like other items, must be dealt with realistically. Here's how to keep them under control.

● Get rid of broken, useless, or out-of-date books. Be especially tough on old textbooks. If you haven't used them in years, you aren't likely to use them at all. If you can find the same material or more current material at the library, you'll need a tremendously convincing reason to justify keeping those old texts.

● If, after simplifying the book collection, you still have a book or stack of books that for one reason or another can't be parted with but doesn't merit shelf space, box them up. List the titles on a 3x5 card and number-code the box and the card. This card will go in your file and the box will go to a remote corner in the basement, garage, attic, or other storage area, where you can forget about it. They will be safe, accessible, and most important, out of the way.

● Arrange what's left in an attractive, eye-catching manner. Group books together according to subject matter rather than size.

Perhaps you've noticed that this is the area in your home that can accommodate ultra-personal decorating touches. Here is where your son's framed stamp collection or an antique, pieced quilt can hang; your spinning wheel or loom plus a basket of hand-spun yarn can sit; or your vast assortment of framed family photos can be displayed. Even though any of this would do well in the living room, the implied cozy comfiness of the family room seems to suit it better.

Making some adjustments in the room you REALLY live in will turn an area that often looks as though nobody cares into a cozy, inviting, yet in-control "make-yourself-at-home" room.

Making Your Kitchen Measure Up

Now for the big one. The room you can't wait to simplify, yet dread starting on. Your family's private fast-food center, dining hall, and gathering place. The kitchen.

The kitchen, after all, is a food and people station, usually the busiest room in the house—in short, the hub of the home. It's a multipurpose area, with many demands placed upon it. Even the list that follows may not present the whole story. A kitchen is a:

√ Storage depot for food, utensils, and equipment
√ Key work center for food preparation and cleanup
√ Area of the home where food is most often eaten
√ Social center
√ Information center
√ Office center
√ Place to do homework
√ Hobby center
√ Small-scale cannery

Because it's such a busy place, it's always being undone; it never stays clean and orderly for long. An overloaded, out-of-control kitchen is self-defeating; maintaining it is time-, energy-, and spirit-consuming. You've probably noticed that it is not only stressful to you, but can be difficult for others to deal with also. That's pretty much why the kitchen needs to be streamlined down to the bare bones: People + kitchen activities + overload = mess, confusion, and lack of control. Eliminating the overload reduces the mess factor, removes much of the confusion, and increases the control people have over this area. So for a kitchen that "measures up" to the demands placed on it, give it a thorough streamlining.

Streamlining the overloaded kitchen means dealing with more than drawers and cupboards. It means getting everything off the countertops and permanently placing these things inside their respective centers. It means a bare minimum (ideally nothing) on the work area walls, that is, the walls above and surrounding all counters and large appliances. Kitchens and their contents accumulate greasy dust and fly specks; they are visually busy because the walls are cut up by cupboards, window, appliances, and entry ways. Hanging anything on these walls creates more work because hung items need frequent washing; what's more, even the cleanest collection can look cluttered at the tilt of a mug.

Streamlining the kitchen also involves removing everything from the window sill and refrigerator top—and keeping these spots clear. We suggest you clear off your refrigerator door as much as possible for easier cleaning. Your office and information centers might be better places for much of this material. Child-related items can be displayed on your laundry or sewing area wall, the inside of a nonpainted cupboard door, the outside or inside of a closet door, on the end of a bank of nonpainted cupboards, or on a specially designated, kitchen-hung cork board. And, if there are open soffits, clear everything off them, too.

GETTING STARTED

Our standard dictionary says a center is a place or point at which a specific activity is concentrated. This is exactly what a kitchen center is: cleanup takes place at the cleanup center, or the sink area; cooking happens at the cooking center, or the stove area, and so on. So to get started, look closely at your living patterns. Assess what happens in your kitchen, then decide what you want to happen there. Plan centers around the latter, not the former.

So STEP 1 is to write these centers down and post them somewhere for quick reference. These choices will be your guide for how you organize what's left after streamlining.

The *typical* kitchen, though not necessarily yours, has a tableware center, cooking center, baking center, cleanup center, and pantry area; these are the basics. More and more have a microwave center, too. If anyone packs a lunch or if there are older children who work in the kitchen, a sandwich center might be in order. Most kitchens house a phone, which means the need for an information center. If you use the kitchen table or a built-in desk for menu planning, bill paying, and checkbook balancing, then you will need a mini-office center. (This is also where incoming mail is handled daily.) Your kitchen may even need more centers—this depends on your lifestyle, available space, and what you want to happen in this area.

Several homemakers we've worked with wanted a snack center. This amounted to a drawer or two for chips, crackers, pretzels, nuts, dried fruits, and so on. A farmhouse kitchen we streamlined needed a dairy center to accommodate the equipment and utensils used in the family milking business. Two popular super-specialized centers are a liquor center and a popcorn center. You can see that kitchen centers have as much variety as the people who work in them.

With centers listed, it's time to begin the actual physical process of simplifying the kitchen.

STEP 2 involves emptying your entire kitchen—all drawers, cupboards, pantry, countertops, refrigerator top, window sills, and even broom closet and tops of soffits. As you are emptying, place contents in logical groupings (dishes and table-related items in one pile, pots and pans in another, and so on). This is where it gets overwhelming—facing a never-ending sea of things and wondering where to put them all. Don't panic; there *will* be a proper place for everything you decide to keep. You will be filling garbage, charity, and "someplace else" bags or boxes to the brim, which will mean much less to put away. So keep going: this system works.

STEP 3 is a little easier. Vacuum and wipe out all drawers, cupboards, pantry, and so on. This is the time to add fresh shelf paper, if you use it.

STEP 4 is to establish the location of all your centers, using your list. Begin with tableware, then cooking, then baking, then cleanup, then pantry, then microwave (if this applies). Remember, though, nothing is set in stone.

You may change your mind here and there, and do some center juggling. That's O.K. We have streamlined hundreds of kitchens, and every time, we've changed our minds about some center locations. Fiddle around with it until you get it just right.

Now it's time to load your centers. The following information will help set up the basics, plus any other centers your lifestyle calls for.

TABLEWARE CENTER

This houses everything that is table related. For example:

- Dishes
- Glasses
- Pretty serving bowls (not plastic refrigerator keepers, microwave dishes, or mixing bowls—which will go someplace else)
- Flatware
- Table linens (placemats, tablecloths, napkins, napkin rings)
- Salt and pepper shakers
- Attractive butter dish
- Table trivets
- Napkin holder
- Sugar bowl
- Jam pot
- Honey and syrup containers

Add to or subtract from this list as it applies to you.

This center should be located closest to your table, not necessarily closest to your dishwasher. Place settings can sit in a cupboard, and flatware, in a drawer. However, if there is no drawer available, place the tray of flatware on the cupboard shelf beside the place settings. Keep an open mind on this suggestion. While it may strike you as inconvenient at first, the extra drawer space it gives you may be worth it. It bears repeating: In this space-crunched world, not everything can be at fingertip reach—sometimes we must endure a little inconvenience for the sake of order and control.

Be selective as you fill this center. No more chipped, cracked, stained, or ugly dishes on your table. No more dingy, plastic, mismatched, or commercial-type glasses at the table. Try to have only matching glassware at all place settings (this is a real morale booster). Set aside five or six plastic or mismatched glasses for use as drink-of-water glasses. These glasses take only a small space near the sink or refrigerator. Put them in a drawer, where they can be laid flat, or in a sliver of available cupboard space. All our clients have liked this drink-of-water glasses system because it keeps the table glasses free and clean for meals.

The salt and pepper, sugar bowl, butter dish, syrup and honey pots, and so on go in the cupboard with your place settings. It is convenient to group them onto a little, round turntable, but if space doesn't permit this, then simply line them up along one wall of the tableware cupboard. Can you see how much convenience is created by having all your table items grouped together? (Actually, nothing is new under the sun. Restaurants have been using this system for a hundred years.)

If you have young children capable of doing kitchen duty, consider putting dishes and glasses in the bottom cupboard closest to the table. This strategy alleviates the cupboard climbing and lessens chances for dish disasters. To keep baby/toddler fingers from destroying or being injured by the contents of cupboards and drawers, use child-proof plastic locks, available in hardware and discount stores.

COOKING CENTER

This should be next to the stove and usually involves a couple of drawers, an upper cupboard, and a lower cupboard.

The upper cupboard, most frequently located above the stove, holds:

- Salt and pepper shakers. (This set, separate from the one in your tableware center, will add convenience to your cooking routine.)
- All cooking herbs. (There's a difference between what is used for baking and what is used for cooking; you don't bake a cake with sage and you don't cook up a spaghetti sauce with cinnamon.) Less-used herbs should not take up valuable kitchen space. Store these in your pantry or general food storage area. "Cooking center" herbs are those used several times a week. NOTE: If you're a cooking "purist," and are concerned about stove heat and fumes affecting the flavor of your herbs, then find another convenient spot for them. Just be sure they are as near the stove as possible.
- Cornstarch
- Gravy and sauce packets (nested neatly and conveniently in a container)
- Pastas
- Bouillon and hot-drink mixes
- Cooked cereals
- Small bottle of vegetable oil. (Keep larger container in pantry and refill as necessary; this goes for all staples—small sizes in your centers and large sizes in your pantry.)
- Parmesan cheese
- Parsley flakes
- Chopped dried onions
- Boxed convenience dinner mixes (if there's room; otherwise, place them in the pantry)

> To control spaghetti, put it in a spaghetti-sized drawstring bag. Make one or purchase one from a kitchen boutique. If you need to conserve space, hang the bag on the inside of a cupboard door or on the inside cupboard wall.

If space is really tight, store less frequently used ingredients in the pantry or food storage area.

The drawers of this center, ideally one on each side of

the stove, house nice pot holders and cooking utensils. Use drawer dividers to arrange the latter. The basic stove utensils are:

- Wire whisk
- Pair of tongs
- Rubber spatula
- Large spoon
- Metal turner
- Plastic turner
- Meat fork
- Two wooden spoons

In almost every instance, you only need one of something. This is a safe number—any more than one of each utensil encourages overload. If you're convinced you need more than one of something, try washing the single utensil and reusing it. Work this way for twenty-one days and see if the little inconvenience isn't worth the extra space and order in your utensil drawer.

> Save time and tears by chopping onions in a blender. Section the onion, fill the blender with cold water, turn on the grate button for two or three seconds. Drain in colander. Spread chopped onion on cookie sheets and flash freeze. Then put in freezer bags and store in the freezer.

Almost every kitchen utensil can be hung. If you're really low on drawer space, then hang some of your utensils inside a cupboard wall or door of your cooking center, and group any nonhanging utensils in a container and set them in the potholder drawer. It is possible to put small finish nails into very thin cupboard doors, if they are carefully pounded in at a severe angle. An alternative to pounding finish nails is to use small plastic hooks with strong, stick-on backs; they're available in the housewares department of discount or department stores. Do *not* hang them on the wall above your stove or on another open wall.

97

Be ruthless when deciding what to keep. In defense of chucking the broken, worn-out, rusty, chewed-up utensils, we've compiled a comparative price list for replacements. (All figures are approximate.)

Metal ladle	$1.97	Tongs	$1.29
Large slotted spoon	$1.59	Plastic spatula	$ .97
Rubber spatula	$ .79	Pancake turner	$1.99
Wooden spoons	3/$ .99	Large metal spoon	$1.59
Potato masher	$1.79	Large wire whisk	$1.99- $2.89

Make a list of utensils that need replacing, and if it's not immediately possible to restock this entire drawer, replace one item at a time. Kitchen work is more fun, even for the "I hate to cook" folks, when there is nice equipment to work with.

The lower cupboard of the cooking center holds:

- Pots
- Pans
- A few carefully chosen appliances such as the Crock-Pot, electric griddle, and frypan. Store detachable cords, wound and secured, with the appliance they go with. Either lay them inside these appliances, or hang them up along the inside of the cupboard door or wall.

Anything in this center is used for cooking, not baking.

We consistently see kitchens loaded with too many pans and appliances. If you want more control and space in your kitchen, get rid of everything but the basics. Why give precious space to a hot dog cooker *and* a saucepan, when the saucepan will not only cook hotdogs, but hundreds of other things as well? Get rid of the hotdog cooker and all other single-purpose, space-eating appliances; keep only the basics. These are:

- One large frypan plus lid

- One Dutch oven (which usually shares the frypan lid). Think this through. If all you use is the electric frypan, you may not want to give space to this Dutch oven.
- One 2-quart saucepan plus lid
- One 1½-quart saucepan plus lid
- One 1-quart saucepan plus lid
- One griddle
- One electric frypan plus lid
- One Crock-Pot plus lid

If you're a quantity cooker, you may need an eight- to ten-quart kettle.

Ideally, pots should be stored with their lids on, but this is probably impractical for most kitchens. Next best is nesting them together and storing them beside the nested lids. If this isn't the best idea for you either, explore your cooking center space for a better way. Hanging as much as possible on inside cupboard walls and doors buys lots of shelf space. Don't overlook the possibility of hanging from the undersides of shelves. However you deal with it, just remember to group like items together and keep only the basic cooking-related things in your cooking center.

Seasonal cooking utensils like the turkey roaster and canning equipment and supplies will be stored someplace else, away from prime kitchen space, probably in your designated storage area (see Chapter 17). Here's a tip regarding canning supplies: After a canning jar is emptied and washed, put a new lid on, upside down, plus the screw band and store. This sytem keeps you one year ahead on all lids, and saves time and effort when you're canning, because there's no need to hunt for and match lids to jars. It will also save you space—because the new lids are stored on the jar, there's no need to sacrifice space for lid storage. You will need a spot in your kitchen for a supply of canning lids (stored in a small box or drawstring bag)—preferably in a cleanup center drawer or under the sink. Be sure to number-code any boxes containing your seasonal kitchen storage things.

BAKING CENTER

This center involves an upper and lower cupboard; the countertop is used only as a work surface, not a resting place for canisters and the like. This is best located between the stove and sink. If you have a galley or corridor kitchen (that is, two banks of cupboards and appliances with a walkway between them), then locate the baking center next to the sink and directly opposite the stove. The other kitchen arrangements—L-shaped, U-shaped, and one-wall—also adapt to the baking center idea.

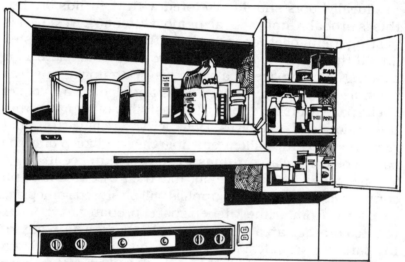

Spices, flavorings, colorings, and mixes are stored in a baking center's upper cupboard.

The upper cupboard inventory should include:

- All sweeteners (brown, powdered, and white sugar; corn syrup; honey; molasses; and so on)
- Shortening
- Flour
- Cornmeal
- Vegetable oil (in small bottle)
- Baking soda
- Baking powder

100

- Salt
- Vanilla and other flavorings (in a container or on a turntable)
- Raisins
- Nuts (if space is limited, they also store well in the freezer)
- Coconut
- Cocoa
- Oatmeal
- Baking chips
- Food colorings
- Spices (in a container or on a turntable)
- Toothpicks
- Mixes
- One four-cup measuring container
- Mixing bowls (three graduated sizes, if there is room; otherwise, they will go in the bottom baking cupboard)

The upper cupboard inventory also includes a few utensils which can be hung on the door or inside wall, or from underneath a cupboard shelf from hooks:

- One wooden spoon
- One set measuring spoons
- One set measuring cups
- One rubber spatula
- Pastry blender
- Pastry brush
- Hand mixer plus cord (examine any hand mixer and you'll find a built-in hole—it's made for hanging)
- Beaters for hand mixer

The lower cupboard inventory should include:

- Baking pans and sheets
- Rolling pin and pastry cloth
- Cooling racks
- Large counter-type mixer plus attachments such as bread hook (hang what you can)

- Cake decorating equipment (in a container)
- Cookie cutters (in a container)

Note that we suggest using containers for several items. They encourage control. Shortening cans, old canisters, shoeboxes, baskets, and old lunch boxes are alternate suggestions to the usual store-bought type. Think "hang" and "containers" and buy yourself more space and control.

> Speaking of baking: Save your twelve- and six-ounce frozen-juice cans. Fill them with a variety of cookie doughs, then cover the open tops with plastic wrap, secured with elastics, and freeze until baking time. When you're ready, let the mixture thaw a bit, then cut the bottom of the can off and use it to push dough up through the can for quick, even slicing.

What do you do if you don't have upper or lower cupboard space for a baking center? You improvise. One of our clients was painfully low on kitchen space. She had only four small upper cupboards, four small shallow drawers, and the space under her sink. (She was lucky enough to have a drawer in her stove, though.) So rather than devote the stove drawer to pots and pans, she put her mixing bowls and all her bakeware there. This drawer approximated a lower cupboard, and was close to her upper baking cupboard. Her pots, pans, and lids could be hung, so she hung them from floor to ceiling on the inside walls of a tiny broom closet that was next to her stove and close to the upper cooking cupboard.

CLEANUP CENTER

This area includes the sink, plus the cupboard directly underneath, and usually a drawer to one side of the sink. The sink needs no inventory: Remove everything from the top except the two plugs. No more plastic scrubbers and scouring pads, no more gummy bars of soap, no more ratty dish rag, no more ceramic big-mouthed frog, and so on. These things go someplace else. This someplace else would probably be under the sink in a container (cleaning bucket or plastic dish tub, perhaps). Or the scrubber and dish rag could hang on the inside cupboard door or inside cupboard wall from small hooks or finish nails. Any sink, porcelain or stainless steel, is easier to clean and keep clean if it's clear—it looks nicer, too.

The purpose of the cleanup center is more than washing dishes or storing household cleaners. It's also a place where fresh fruits and vegetables are handled, cooked pastas are rinsed and drained, canning jars are assembled for storage, and beverages are prepared. In short, it's really a multipurpose center.

The underneath cupboard is a fun space to work with—you can really be clever here. Empty everything out and assess. The typical sink cupboard has way too much unneeded stuff in it, and it's dark. Consider giving its walls and floor a coat of high-gloss, white enamel. This will brighten up the area and make cleaning it easier. One of our clients went a step further and had a cut-to-fit piece of Formica laid on the bottom of this cupboard.

Again, hang as much as possible, on cupboard doors, inside walls of cupboards, even from the underside of the countertop. A cleaning-products shelf can be created from a board, in the back of the cupboard.

Keep in mind that you probably don't need most of the cleaning products you currently stock. Take Don Aslett's advice and buy four or five commercial plastic spray bottles; purchase your disinfectants and cleaners in concentrated gallons. (These are found at any janitorial supply.) Follow mixing directions given on container labels, and label each bottle. You'll get dollars' worth of cleaner for pennies an ounce, and the spray bottles will take up less space under your sink (store the gallon jugs in your general storage area—described in Chapter 17).

Streamlining your cleaning products collection will leave a lot of open space that will be put to better use. For example, sitting in a cleaning bucket under Alice's sink

are a spray bottle of ammonia water, a commercial squeegee, an old toothbrush, a treated dust cloth, a clean three-
inch paintbrush, and five cleaning cloths. The ammonia
water and squeegee are used for windows. The toothbrush
cleans hard-to-get-at places like faucet crevices. The cleaning cloths, as opposed to rags, are for the big, tough cleaning jobs like floor scrubbing. The paintbrush is great for
dusting pleated lamp shades, mitered cupboard doors and
picture frames, cupboard hardware, intricate woodwork,
and so on. (For much more about cleaning, we refer you to
several fine books listed under "Suggested Reading" at the
end of this book.)

The lower part of a cleanup center is located under the sink.

Basically, your under-sink inventory looks like this:

- Dish soap. (Use a tiny squirt of this to wash your hands before handling food; this eliminates the need for gummy bar
  soap on top of the sink.) If your sink is the community wash
  trough, consider rerouting others to the laundry or bathroom sinks for their grubby cleanup. Look at all areas of the
  kitchen in terms of food preparation and high sanitation
  needs. Keep the sink as clean and sanitary as possible.

- Dishwasher detergent
- Household cleaning products—the bare essentials. For safety reasons, you may want to put cleaners out of reach of little fingers, but if lack of space causes you to put them under the sink, child-proof locks on the doors should keep this area secure.
- Good window squeegee
- Cleaning bucket, with aforementioned basic supplies tucked inside
- Dish drainer. Hang it on the inside wall or door, or stand it up, along the side wall. Consider standing up flat items such as cookie and pizza pans, trays, cutting board, on their sides next to the drainer, if you have no slotted tray cupboard; you can improvise a tray cupboard to fit the space under the sink.
- Colander(s), hung on inside wall or door (put a hole in the rim for hanging, if necessary)
- Plunger. You might want it under a bathroom sink, but whichever sink it sits under, it'll do so more easily if you shorten the handle.
- New canning lids in a small box or drawstring bag (which, of course, could be hung up)
- Simple tool kit. (This could also sit in the cupboard over the refrigerator, or in an empty drawer. Don't overlook the possibility of drawstring-bagging the contents.) The kit should include a screwdriver, a Phillips screwdriver, a pair of pliers, a small hammer, a small container of finish nails, and super glue.
- Shoeshine kit. (This could also go in the utility or laundry area, depending on where shoes are shined; the bedroom, however, is not the place for this dirty job.) Tuck some newspaper inside the container for use as a drop cloth.
- Paper towels could go on the inside of the door. If you have a microwave, a handier place would be on the wall between the sink and microwave—an exception to the "nothing-on-the-work-area walls" doctrine.
- If there's no better out-of-the-way place for the garbage, then under the sink it goes, in a plastic container; a doorhung container is best, because it frees space on the cupboard floor.
- A nice dish cloth, dish towel, and hand towel hung on rods attached to the inside door. (Another spot for these might be the end of a bank of cupboards.)

The under-sink area is prone to overload, mostly because of cleaning products. So when you stock this area, work toward "efficient" rather than "full."

The drawer to the side of the sink holds:

- Five or six dish cloths
- Five or six dish towels
- A few decorative hand towels
- A couple of aprons
- Bibs, if this applies

If you're without available drawer space, these items could rest neatly in a plastic dish tub under the sink.

PANTRY

This depends on available space and where you've housed your other centers; it's a minimal storage spot and not a work center, so the pantry area will use any leftover kitchen space, or it could even be in a closet close to the kitchen. (Streamlining makes such spaces available.) One mobile home kitchen we simplified had no leftover space for the pantry, so the homemaker installed shelves in the living room closet, immediately around the corner from the kitchen, and stocked it with back-up supplies of staples.

This area is considered a minimal storage center because it usually is not big enough to hold bulk sizes or large quantities of things. It's the place for selected amounts of:

- Canned goods
- Dry cereals
- Crackers
- Convenience mixes
- Fruit-flavored gelatins
- A few back-up supplies (salt box, large bottle of vegetable oil, occasionally used herbs and spices)

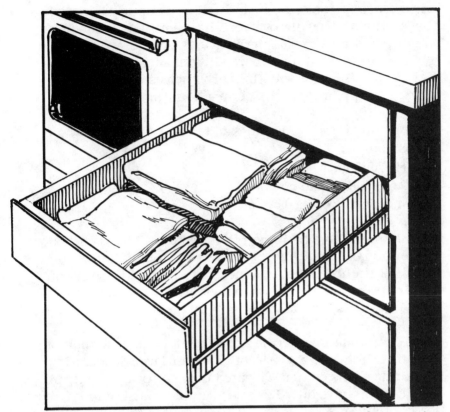

Store kitchen linens, aprons, and bibs in the drawer of your cleanup center.

It all depends on available space, but thinking of your pantry area as the place for your one- to two-week food supplies and the storage area as the place for longer-term food supplies will make it easier to position this center.

MORE FROM CENTRAL PLANNING

Your lifestyle determines the kinds of centers in your kitchen, so you'll pick and choose from this chapter. We have four more suggestions, though, that can add extra convenience and efficiency to any kitchen.

  • If you have a microwave, then you need a microwave

center. Ideally, it should be located in a cupboard directly above or below the microwave, if it's a countertop model. If you have a built-in wall microwave, the center would be in the closest adjacent cupboard. If your microwave is on a cart, put the center on the cart shelves directly underneath the appliance. This center houses:

- All microwave-safe cooking and baking dishes
- Carousel
- Thermometer
- Paper plates and napkins
- Microwave cookbook and recipes

We once simplified a kitchen that just didn't have an available cupboard to devote to microwave items. So we combined all the microwave dishes onto a shelf in the tableware cupboard. (The homemaker also uses these microwave dishes as her table serving dishes.)

- A sandwich center or lunch center needs a shelf or two either above or below a counter, or a large deep drawer. It's handy if this center is located near the built-in cutting board, if you have one. The space must be large enough to accommodate:

- A toaster (set in a shoebox lid or some other improvised tray to catch crumbs)
- Bread goods
- Peanut butter (unless it's the old-fashioned kind, in which case it must be stored in the refrigerator)
- Margarine

If anyone packs a lunch, this area also houses:

- Lunch box(es)
- Food wraps
- Sandwich bags
- Paper lunch sacks

- Lunch-box containers (Thermos, small serving cups with tight-fitting lids, and so on)
- Plastic flatware
- Paper napkins

Even if your lifestyle doesn't call for a sandwich center, you should keep the toaster off the counter. Putting it into a cupboard or drawer near the place you use it would be best. We've streamlined hundreds of kitchens, and in every instance, clear countertops ranked as the favorite aspect of it all (an efficient baking center ranked second).

- An information center is an automatic need if your kitchen has a phone. Obviously, the center should be near the phone; it could be a drawer, shelf, or just a cork bulletin board or washable message board.

The items needed for this center are few. They include:

- Phone book
- Calendar for scheduling
- Pencil
- Notepad for messages
- Tacks for posting messages
- Washable message board *or* bulletin board

Use ingenuity here. If you have lots of drawer or shelf space, borrow some for this center. If there's no drawer or shelf, then the wall surrounding the phone is the answer (most kitchen phones are wall-mounted). One family surrounded their phone with a sturdy cork bulletin board out of which a phone-sized piece had been cut out. If you do this, tack the notepad to the board; tape a string to a pencil and tack the stringed pencil and calendar up also. If yours is a small phone book, and it would be handier to hang it, then open it to the middle, lay a sturdy cord down the center of the back, shut the book, tie the two cord ends together, and you have looped your book for hanging. If you just use a washable message board, the need for notepad and pencil is eliminated, but you'll still need a handy place for the calendar and phone book. Incidentally,

109

Arrange your information center around the phone.

don't slap a calendar, no matter how pretty the pictures, up on the wall as you would a framed picture. Calendars are service items and rarely do well as part of wall decor. Better to mount it inside a cupboard door, closet door, or on the end of a bank of cupboards.

● The office center is the last of our suggestions. This center is a combination-location center: a shelf or drawer

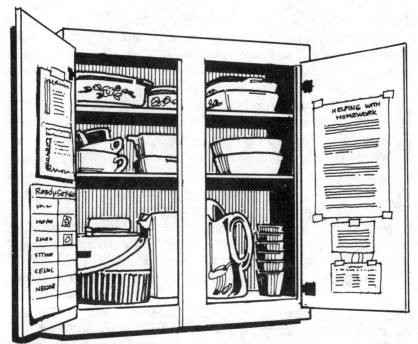

If space is scarce, use the insides of cupboard doors to extend your information center.

near the table, or a portable file box and the kitchen table itself, unless you're one of the lucky ones with a specific office-designated room or a built-in kitchen desk. Your office center is where bill paying, checkbook balancing, menu planning, letter writing, and handling of incoming mail take place. The shelf, drawer, or file box holds the necessary items for all this:

- Pen and pencil
- Address book
- Stationery
- Small calendar
- Notebook paper
- Checkbook
- Office supplies
- "To do" file folder
- Budget book

The "to do" file folder is the place to put bills that need paying, letters that need answering, and the food ads from the current week's newspaper (unless you can deal with these immediately after arrival of the newspaper). These grocery-sale ads will help you compose your weekly menu. If chicken is on sale, for example, then chicken is a logical choice for an evening meal or the weekend barbeque and perhaps for sandwiches for one day's lunches. If there's a good buy on bananas, then this is what you'll buy plenty of, rather than lots of apples, which could be considerably more expensive. From this weekly menu, you will write your grocery list. This is a slick system because you'll not only save money by avoiding impulse and desperation purchases, but you'll also save in-store time—no more wandering and pondering over what to fix for dinner.

The papers brought in from school that need signing don't go there, however. Deal with school papers as soon as they enter the house, or as soon as you enter the house. Have the children wash out and dry their lunch boxes while you're looking their things over. Then sign what needs signing, tuck it into the clean lunch box to be transported the next day, and forget about it. (This technique takes care of the "Hurry and sign my papers, the bus is coming!" scramble that so many mornings can witness.)

While we're not experts on papers and filing, we do have one tip: On the way into the house with the mail, stop off at the garbage can to deposit all junk mail. This keeps the in-house paper piles much smaller.

LEFTOVERS THAT AREN'T OVERLOAD

There are five categories of kitchen items that still need some attention. First of all, your general utensils need a home all their own. (General utensils are anything you don't cook or bake with, such as the hand can opener, ice cream scoop, nutcracker, pie server, bottle opener, and so on.) If there's an empty drawer, then in they go, probably in a drawer organizer. If there isn't an empty drawer, group them into a container, and find a vacant spot in some already occupied drawer.

Some words on the electric can opener: If you love it and routinely use it, keep it—but keep it off the counter. You will find some drawer it can sit in or some shelf or cupboard it can sit on. Even if you use it fourteen times a day, we still say get it off the counter. Clear surfaces are worth any inconvenience created: they make for easy maintenance, allow your decorator touches to finally be noticed, make a room look cleaner and bigger, instill vigor, inspiration, enthusiasm. . . . Need we go on? If you don't routinely use it and feel you could get along with the hand can opener, fine—discard the electric one.

Next, what about knives and other cutting tools, such as the cheese slicer or the pizza wheel? Don't hang them on the wall or set them in a knife block on the counter. If they are keepers, put them in a drawer, *in containers*, perhaps in their own cardboard sleeves (for blade and sharpness preservation).

Third, what to do with all those plastic bowls and lids? First of all, sort through them and keep only four or five plus matching lids, in graduating sizes. All should be in tip-top shape. When these bowls are full of leftovers, then it's time to empty them out and serve potluck for dinner.

Rather than nest these bowls inside one another and plop the lids somewhere else, place a lid on each bowl and stack them, two bowls per stack, or whatever your cupboard space allows. They will sit neatly in a cupboard (the best place is near the cleanup center or refrigerator). Keep them separate from serving and mixing bowls.

What about cookbooks and recipes? After you've streamlined these, too, place the keepers in or near one of several places: the baking center, the cooking center, or the office-planning center (if this center is in the kitchen).

Finally, what do you do with the broom, dustpan, and mop? Most homemakers own this equipment, yet most homes have little or no space to accommodate them. The ideal would be a work or janitorial closet just off the kitchen, large enough to house all your cleaning machines and supplies. But since this ideal is rare, we have some alternative suggestions.

● If you have a door between the garage and the kitchen, hang them on the garage wall, just outside the door.

● If there's access to the wall behind the refrigerator, pull it out three to four inches and hang the items up behind the refrigerator. Use spring-type clamps for the broom and mop; hang the whisk broom and dustpan from hooks inserted into the underside of the cupboard above the refrigerator, if there is one. The same principle applies if there's access to a side wall beside the refrigerator.

● If there is a hall closet off the kitchen (maybe the guest coat closet), designate one end wall as the broom and mop center and hang these there.

● If there's a stairway off the kitchen leading down to the basement, hang the broom, mop, dustpan, and so on, on one stairway wall.

● Wherever you put them, be sure to hang them up. This is cleaner and more convenient, and it preserves broom bristles.

TAKE NOTE

It's helpful to understand, as you're assigning things to each center, that there are three categories of utensils in a kitchen: cooking (such as the meat fork and large slotted spoon), baking (such as measuring cups and pastry blender), and general (such as the hand can opener and ice cream scoop).

There are four categories of bowls in a kitchen: serving (which are usually glass or ceramic), mixing (which are plastic, glass, or metal), microwave-safe (which are usually ceramic), and refrigerator keepers (which are glass or plastic).

While filling trash and charity bags, consider putting duplicates and not-needed items into an "apartment box," if you have someone in the family who will eventually strike out on his or her own. This box would be labeled and placed in storage until the event.

LAST BUT NOT LEAST

With everything streamlined, centers pinpointed and stocked, and leftovers dealt with, it's time to deal with walls. As we stated earlier, the kitchen is the place to keep things extra simple. Put nothing on work area walls. Hang nothing along your soffits. This means less to clean, less time for maintenance, less clutter, less visual confusion.

If you enjoy decorator touches such as baskets, plants, pottery, brass and so on, here and there in your kitchen, remember what we said in the living room chapter: Decorative accents get buried in clutter. Keep the kitchen streamlined and your decorating will be easily noticed and really will enhance the room.

As for the rest of the kitchen walls, use the basic principles of design. You and your family spend lots of time in the kitchen, so take this opportunity to create a "special" kitchen—one that really "measures up."

CENTER:	Tableware	Cooking	Baking	Cleanup
Location:	In cupboard and drawer closest to table	In upper, lower cupboard and drawers next to stove	Upper and lower cupboard including counter between sink and stove	Sink and underneath cupboard, plus one drawer to side of sink
Basic Inventory:	dishes glassware serving bowls flatware table linens salt and pepper butter dish sugar bowl honey and jam pots syrup container trivets paper napkins paper plates and cups (seasonal) napkin rings	pastas cooking herbs salt and pepper cornstarch packaged mixes cooked cereals bouillon and hot-drink mixes garlic seasoned salt pot holders tongs wire whisk rubber spatula metal pancake turner wooden spoon large slotted spoon large spoon meat fork pots, pans plus lids Crock-Pot griddle electric frypan parsley dried, chopped onions	baking soda, baking powder all sweeteners shortening vegetable oil salt vanilla and other flavorings flour raisins, nuts, coconut oatmeal cocoa unsweetened chocolate baking chips spices toothpicks food colorings convenience mixes (cake, muffin, and so on) mixing bowls wooden spoon measuring spoons measuring cups one 4-cup measuring cup mixer and beaters rubber spatula pastry blender baking pans and sheets rolling pin and pastry cloth cooling racks cake-decorating equipment cookie cutters pastry brush	paper towels dish soap scouring pad plastic scouring pad dishwasher detergent dish drainer LinSol wood cleaner cleaning bucket cleaning cloths old toothbrush ammonia water in spray bottle oven cleaner 2- to 3-inch clean paintbrush 5 or 6 dish cloths 5 or 6 dish towels 4 or 5 hand towels 3 or 4 aprons new canning lids simple tool kit plunger (?) colander

CENTER:	Information	Sandwich	Microwave	Pantry
Location:	Drawer or shelf near phone, or the wall surrounding the phone	Two shelves either above or below the counter, or deep drawer(s)	One or two shelves above, below, or near microwave	Two shelves or separate pantry or closet at least near the kitchen
Basic Inventory:	phone book pen and pencil notepad or washable message board calendar tacks	toaster bread goods peanut butter (unless it's old-fashioned, in which case it must be stored in refrigerator) margarine lunch boxes plastic wraps and other food wraps sandwich bags paper lunch sacks lunch-box containers	cooking and baking dishes (microwave-safe) thermometer carousel microwave cook book, recipes paper plates paper napkins	canned goods backup supplies (vegetable oil, salt box, and so on) dry cereals gelatins convenience mixes crackers

CENTER:	Office
Location:	Shelf, drawer, or portable file box near table area; or built-in kitchen desk or other such designated room
Basic Inventory:	pens and pencils address book stationery "to do" file folder budget book small calendar office supplies notebook paper stamps checkbook business-size envelopes

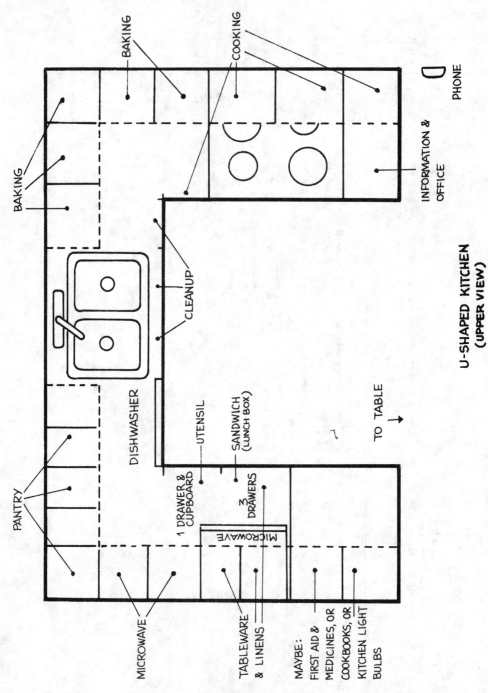

BAKING

BAKING

BAKING

COOKING

PHONE

INFORMATION & OFFICE

CLEANUP

DISHWASHER

UTENSIL

SANDWICH (LUNCH BOX)

TO TABLE →

1 DRAWER & CUPBOARD

3 DRAWERS

MICROWAVE

PANTRY

MICROWAVE

TABLEWARE & LINENS

MAYBE:

FIRST AID & MEDICINES, OR

COOKBOOKS, OR

KITCHEN LIGHT BULBS

U-SHAPED KITCHEN
(UPPER VIEW)

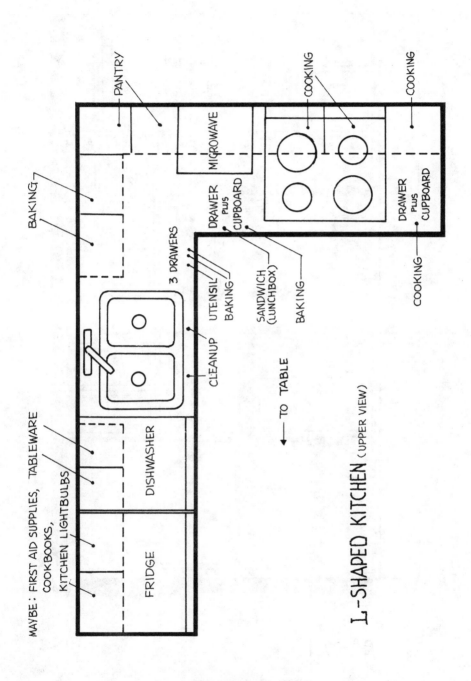

MAYBE: FIRST AID SUPPLIES, TABLEWARE
COOKBOOKS,
KITCHEN LIGHTBULBS

BAKING

PANTRY

FRIDGE

DISHWASHER

3 DRAWERS

CLEANUP

UTENSIL
BAKING

DRAWER
PLUS
CUPBOARD

SANDWICH
(LUNCHBOX)

BAKING

MICROWAVE

COOKING

COOKING

DRAWER
PLUS
CUPBOARD

COOKING

→ TO TABLE

L-SHAPED KITCHEN (UPPER VIEW)

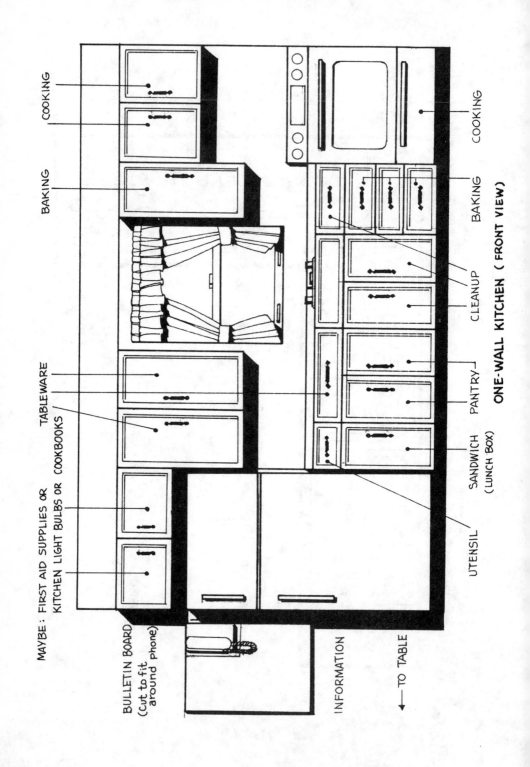

ONE-WALL KITCHEN (FRONT VIEW)

COOKING

BAKING

CLEANUP

PANTRY

SANDWICH
(LUNCH BOX)

UTENSIL

COOKING

BAKING

TABLEWARE

MAYBE: FIRST AID SUPPLIES OR
KITCHEN LIGHT BULBS OR COOKBOOKS

BULLETIN BOARD
(Cut to fit
around phone)

INFORMATION

◄— TO TABLE

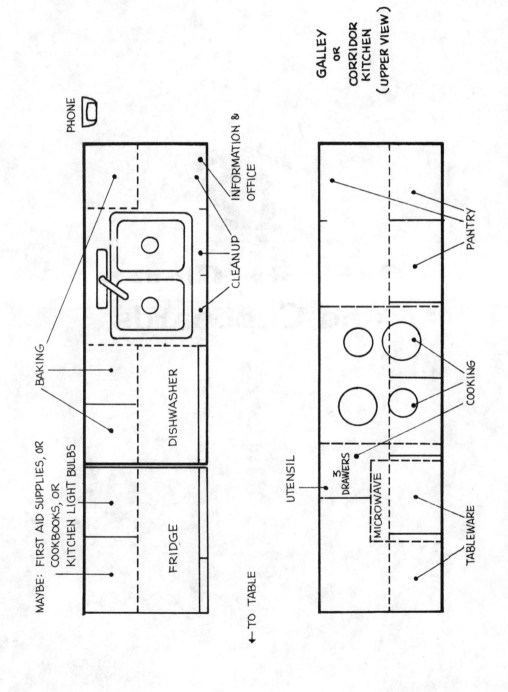

PHONE

GALLEY
OR
CORRIDOR
KITCHEN
(UPPER VIEW)

INFORMATION &
OFFICE

CLEANUP

BAKING

MAYBE: FIRST AID SUPPLIES, OR
COOKBOOKS, OR
KITCHEN LIGHT BULBS

DISHWASHER

FRIDGE

← TO TABLE

PANTRY

COOKING

UTENSIL

3
DRAWERS

MICROWAVE

TABLEWARE

12

Cabinets, Closets, and Cupboards

Cabinets, closets, and cupboards are almost interchangeable in function, and they're very close by definition, too. According to one standard dictionary, a cabinet is a case or cupboard, usually one with doors and shelves. A cupboard is a closet with shelves, usually where dishes, utensils, or food is kept. And a closet is a cabinet or recess for china, household utensils, or clothes.

Whatever you call these indispensable storage zones— and that varies by region and family—they're probably very full of all the things mentioned in those definitions, and more. Certainly before we simplified our homes, we were constantly struggling for control of our storage areas. We found, however, that it wasn't enough just to organize their contents; we had done that repeatedly, and realized that this temporary type of organization wasn't the answer. We were doing the household shuffle, when all along we should have been using the household shovel. We needed a system that would give us control of our closets and all other spaces in our homes once and for all. Here, as elsewhere in the house, simplifying, then organizing, is the answer. And because you're dealing with relatively small spaces, simplifying is all the more vital.

HALL CLOSETS

You handle hall or hall-type closets just as you would the master bedroom or other bedroom closet. It doesn't matter whether the items in it are coats, china, games, or cleaning supplies. Here are some general pointers.

● Note the closet's location and determine its purpose. Evaluate it with convenience and availability in mind. A closet near the front door may not be the best place for your twice-a-year camping equipment, if that's the only entrance-level closet you have. The space is needed more for coats. If you have a back-door or basement closet, that's a better place for the camping goods; if you don't, consider the garage (and see Chapter 16 for more about that).

123

Food and home-management storage from freed space.

Sports equipment.

● Touch every item in the closet and use those key questions we discussed earlier (see Chapter 3 to refresh your memory). We all burden ourselves with things that have no long-lasting value. Why give prime space—or any space—to things we don't need, don't want, don't use, don't like, and really don't have room for? Don't be tempted to keep inferior items. Limited space should go to only high-quality things. By weeding out nonessentials, you'll find far less to organize. Quality over quantity is always the motto.

• Some prefer centrally locating all games. So if this is the place you've decided to put board games, rather than the children's rooms, then deal with them just as discussed in Chapter 8. Assess their condition and determine if they are worth keeping. Check for broken or missing pieces, which will never return; decide, too, whether the games are still of interest. This type of assessment could whittle your game collection in half.

• Again, group and store like items together. For instance, gather up all costume or children's "dress-up" items and store them in one box; collect all your arts and crafts and needlework projects and put them into one container. Here's a time- and money-saving tip: Keep a box for "gifts"; fill it with all-age, all-occasion prewrapped gifts (each one discreetly labeled so you don't forget what it is). These gifts most likely will be quality after-season sale items. This system ends that last-minute gift hunt we all know and dread.

• Store seasonal things out of the way. This frees space for things of the current season. We once streamlined a closet that was hiding garden seeds, ski boots, and a steam canner. We grouped these things with other related items and stored them away, waiting for the correct season to call them forth.

• Store frequently-used items in handy places—at their place of use whenever possible. For example, we use our mixer/dough-hook/blender appliance three or four times a day, so we need it in a convenient cupboard, out front for quick removal. We use our curling irons at least once every day, so we have them hanging on the inside of the bathroom cabinet door for easy access. We use our typewriters every day, but we use our slide projector only a couple times a month in seminars. So you can see which item gets the prime, convenient space.

It's not always possible to have everything at your fingertips, of course. A little inconvenience may be necessary— but at least store the item as near as possible to its logical place-of-use spot.

• Be fanatical with everyone about putting things back in their assigned spots. Neglect of this can undo any organizational system. This is a realistic expectation once there are plenty of empty spaces and logical assignments for all keepers. Once, it might not have been fair to expect your five-year-old to put Candyland away; even you probably couldn't squeeze another game box onto the game shelf without it all falling on your head. Fear of toppling shelves and exploding drawers prevented everyone but the most fearless from attempting to put things back where they pulled them out from. But this isn't the case anymore.

• Hang as much as possible. Look at the space within the closet—along the back wall, closet ceiling, and other inside walls. These may be feasible areas to hang related items that aren't frequently used but do belong in the closet. For instance, Alice grouped poster paints into a drawstring bag and hung them from the closet ceiling, above the oil-paint box, which sits on the upper shelf.

MORE "NO-LINEN CLOSETOLOGY"

Here's a revolutionary thought: You may not really *need* a linen closet for extra bed linens. Storing them in a linen closet is an extravagant waste of space. In the interest of better space management, get rid of the extra bed linens.

We can't think of a single house we've ever been in that didn't have a linen closet or cupboard, so we conclude that linen closets are an integral ingredient in the American housing concept. This probably explains why we consistently run into stubborn opposition when we introduce this different approach to linen storage. It sounds radical at first, but it frees needed space.

Here's what you do. After assessing the condition of all bed linens, and discarding any that are worn or faded (maybe you can put them in the garage rag bag), pack the rest into a box and store it. Keep only what is currently on the beds, plus an extra set laid flat between box spring and mattress. (If you have a waterbed, store the extra set on the closet shelf or in a drawer.) You may decide to assign a certain color of sheets to each bedroom. If you have small children or a bed-wetter, store a couple of sets of sheets laid flat between the mattresses. Even an extra cold-weather blanket will store well between the mattresses if you lay it flat. When it's time to launder, take the bed linens off, wash and dry them, then return them to their appropriate places. This extra set between the box spring and mattress is basically for emergencies or to be put on the mattress if you can't get the dirty set laundered and put back on in the same day. For a Hide-A-Bed, use the same approach: store a set of sheets and a blanket flat between the folded-up mattress sections, or place the clean bedding directly on the mattress, and store it in the folded-up Hide-A-Bed. If you have extra pillows, box them up and store them away.

There are many uses for extra sheets besides the garage rag bag. They make great costumes, curtains, first-aid kit bandages (when ripped into strips and sterilized), drop cloths, and drawstring bags.

Somewhere in the middle of our "no-linen closet" speech we usually are interrupted with one or both of these comments: "But if the linens aren't rotated, they'll wear out quicker," and "But that's boring. I like a variety of sheets." In reply to the first: we do not have any scientific information to refute it. In fact, it's probably true. But we reason that having the extra, simplified closet space is well worth having the sheets wear out a little sooner. We're convinced this "necessary" linen closet could be put to better use. To the second comment, we can't relate. We'd rather have clear, uncluttered space than a variety of sheets.

Here are some suggestions for space that used to be a linen closet. We recognize that not everyone has a main-floor linen closet; because closet locations are so variable, the usefulness of these ideas will depend on the floor plan of your home.

- Turn it into an arts-and-crafts center, or keep your sewing machine, supplies, and notions there.

127

Sewing closet.   Canning and canned-goods closet.

- Create a mini-office. Alice, for example, does all her writing at the kitchen table, but stores her files, reference books, paper, pencils, and so on in the former linen closet.

- Make it into a children's library/school-book center. One of our clients, with several children living in tiny bedrooms, needed an orderly spot for each child's collection of library books and school books. We emptied the linen closet and assigned one shelf for every two children.

- If you don't have built-in dining room storage, you might find that a china-and-crystal center or a wine-and-liquor center works well here.

- If you're tight on food-storage space, keeping food here may be the answer, either for long-term storage or as an off-kitchen pantry.

- An upstairs linen closet can be converted to an arts-and-crafts center, a library-study center (by installing a table-height shelf, an electrical outlet for a lighting fixture, and a small stool), or a toy-storage area.

CHINA CABINETS OR DINING ROOM BUILT-INS

This spot can be one of the loveliest in the home if it isn't overloaded or used as a drop-off station. Unfortunately, it is here that we've found piles of ratty tablecloths and placemats, wrinkled gift-wrapping paper, melted-beyond-use candles, and drawers full of papers needing filing. Unload it and assess every item, firmly using the key questions.

So that this area can be an efficient amenity rather than a complete detraction, give each cabinet section a specific assignment and then reload it accordingly. Depending on its location, it might be able to serve as your total tableware center, thus freeing up needed kitchen cupboard space. You may find that once you have your china or dining cupboard streamlined, you'll be inclined to use your pretty things on a regular basis, rather than waiting for those few special occasions. Not only is this a fun family treat (breakfast juice in goblets and so on), but it also encourages better table manners.

13

The Case of
the Missing Sock:
The Laundry Area

Washing machines don't really eat socks. And dirty socks don't really get up and walk away. But when desperate searching throughout the house turns up nothing, you do begin to wonder. Creating a more efficient (and naturally more pleasant) laundry area will do a lot to end that ever-recurring mystery.

A laundry area can have many purposes, but the foremost is to wash and dry laundry. Because laundry is a never-ending, cyclic chore, it's crucial that the place you spend so much time in be a cheerful and efficient work center, and not a demoralizing, unproductive torture chamber.

After careful study of many laundry centers, we've come up with this composite sketch of a typically overloaded, inefficient wash-dry spot:

√Dirty laundry piled all over the floor
√Crowded, cluttered dryer top
√Cluttered window sill
√Supplies crammed here and there
√Collections of assorted "empties" around
√Inadequate or nonexistent shelving
√Illogically stocked, overloaded shelves
√Overflowing trash container or no trash container
√Very dusty and dirty machines
√Dirty and dusty floors, window, sill
√Dirty and dusty hot-water tank and furnace
√Bedraggled window curtain or covering
√Bare walls except for fuse box and spider webs
√Dirty laundry sink
√A collection of orphaned screws, bolts, nails, pennies, rocks, marbles . . .

Even the most expensive home is likely to have a laundry center that suffers from inefficient organization and a lifeless appearance. And that contributes to discouragement and irritation over a job that's never done and over a place that's unpleasant to be in. Well, laundry will always be with us, so we need to make the best of it. Accepting drab, dirty, inefficient working conditions is unprofessional and sad, and there's no need to live with a negative laundry situation. A thorough simplifying and cleaning of your laundry area will not only save you time and professionalize your wash-day routine, but also lift your spirits.

What condition is your laundry facility in, and how close to the ideal is it? And what is the ideal, anyway? Well, the ideal is a clean, simplified, bright, functional area with caught-up laundry. Even if your laundry setup suffers from a poor location or does double duty, sharing space with sink and toilet, miscellaneous storage, or a sewing machine, for example, it is possible to achieve this ideal. Try these ideas:

- Keep the window sill clear for easy cleaning.
- Check the window covering: if it isn't attractive and serviceable, change it.
- Create a central laundry-supply area, using shelving. Having supplies grouped together in one spot will save time by streamlining your routine.
- Don't use the dryer top as a catch-all. Keeping it clear and sparkling works magic on the area's overall appearance.
- Create a permanent spot for a continuously filling charity bag. Clothes are a transient affair—always in the process of

An efficient laundry area has shelving for supplies, a clear dryer top, and sparkling-clean surfaces.

wearing out, going out of style, or being grown out of. The laundry area is a logical place to do regular clothes assessment. Don't wait until closets and dressers are bulging with obvious candidates for the charity bag—take care of them as they pass through the laundry.

- Periodically move machines for a thorough floor vacuuming and scrubbing. Go after those elusive dust bunnies.

- Regularly dust and shine all surfaces in the area, even the hot-water tank and furnace. This is especially important if the wash is done in the garage—you need as much sparkle in there as you can get.

- Make sure your area is well lighted.

- Use laundry baskets for sorting dirty laundry rather than piling it on the floor.

- Keep a spray bottle of highly diluted ammonia water solution with laundry supplies. This is good for wiping and shining the machines.

- Keep a bottle of clear vinegar with laundry supplies. Add ½ to 1 cup to the final rinse of the wash load once in a while; it cuts soap buildup.

- Hang a bulletin board nearby so you can post a stain-removal chart, fabric-care labels, and so on.

- Consider hanging the children's Mother's Day and Christmas cards and gifts on a laundry area wall. This brightens things up, and kids like seeing their work on display.

- If yours is a sock-eating machine, try two things: load the socks first, and/or have each person put dirty socks in his own net bag (either purchased or home-sewn). Then just toss socks, bag and all, into machine; they'll come clean without losing mates. Each person is then responsible for pairing up his own socks. (Keep the empty sock bag hanging on a hook inside each bedroom closet, to await more dirty socks.)

- Once your entire home is simplified, allow mateless socks to linger only a couple weeks. If mates don't show up after that time period, junk them and start over with new pairs of socks.

- If there are lots of beds in your house, assign one day of the week to laundering the bedding of one or two at a time. This way you avoid that grueling chore of washing a mountain of bedding.

- Hang the ironing board up.

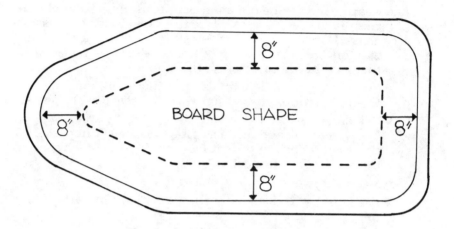

Make your own cover from an old sheet or other large piece of fabric. The pattern is the shape of your board, plus eight inches all around to accommodate the cover wrapping across the top and under the top, plus a two-inch elastic casing. The length of elastic inserted in the two-inch casing should be about half the entire circumference of the board shape. Example: if it is 65" around the shape of a board, the elastic length would be half that, or 32½". Thread the elastic through the casing, stitch ends, and slip the casing over the old pad.

- Have a small basket handy to catch all the pocket paraphernalia that passes through the wash undetected—things like loose change, nails, and nuts and bolts.
- If you buy your detergent in bulk, keep a smaller container of it in the laundry area and house your bulk boxes in your storage area, unless there's ample, efficient space for back-up laundry supplies in your laundry area.
- If there is no shelf available in your laundry area, use hanging wire baskets to hold laundry supplies above the washer. Or add a shelf if there is space available for one.
- Here's a clean-laundry idea that we admit isn't original (we first heard it from Daryl Hoole). Have a labeled laundry tub (which can be a square plastic dish tub) for each person in the family. This is where all clean, folded laundry goes. As-

sign to each individual the responsibility for putting his own folded clothes away and returning the empty tubs to the laundry area.

- In conclusion, one last laundry tip: Keep a sense of humor, especially if there are kids in the house. And if laundry ever gets the best of you, look at it this way: the beauty of living out of the dryer is that it saves space (you don't need dressers) and money (you don't need to buy laundry tubs!).

No More
So-So Sewing Room

A separate room for sewing is every sewer's dream, but it's not always a possibility. Some have only part of a room; others have only a closet for storing the machine and notions, and a kitchen table to sew on. Wherever *you* sew, this chapter is for you.

We love to sew, have done it for years, and know what it's like to sew in an overloaded sewing area. We also know that overload and the resulting clutter can cure you of a love of sewing.

If you're in danger of that kind of cure—if yours is only a so-so sewing area (or not even that)—here are some ways you can simplify and improve it.

PUT AWAY YOUR PATTERNS

Start with your patterns. Watch these, because they pile up fast and go out of style faster. Keep only those that are worth keeping, then file them in a drawer or orange crate. Use categories that apply to your particular sewing habits. For example:

Children's sizes	0-6
Children's	6-10
Girls'	10-14
Girls'	14-18
Men's	all sizes
Women's	all sizes
Dresses	
Sportswear	
Maternity	
Miscellaneous	

Under "Miscellaneous," file patterns for aprons, hats, costumes, and home interior or craft items.

FOLD YOUR FABRICS

Carefully evaluate your fabric supply. Keep only fabric that will look good after it's sewn. If it has permanent creases, faded or out-of-style colors, or is otherwise objectionable or flawed, get rid of it. For example, Alice once bought a pretty piece of single-knit fabric at a terrific price, brought it home, and discovered a large hole and run in the middle. The fabric surrounding the hole and run was not ample enough to be used for much, unless she was making knit potholders, which she wasn't. Of course, you know she kept this piece around for years; after all, she paid good money for it.

Some fabrics rot if kept too long, so watch for this also. When you're deciding what materials to store, remember that cotton blends (especially calico, gingham check, or plaid prints), denims, and nylon tricot are classic fabrics. They are worth saving and storing. Other fabrics, such as knits and polyesters, don't have this longevity, so don't give them long-term space. Whether you store your fabric in a drawer or orange box or on a shelf, indicate the yardage on each piece, so at a glance you can tell how much you have.

If you're an avid seamstress, keep a small swatch booklet of your made-up fabric in your purse. Then, when you are shopping, you can accurately match up a garment to new shoes, other fabrics, accessories, and so on.

NEATEN YOUR NOTIONS

An out-of-control pile of mending constantly bidding for attention is depressing. To eliminate this annoyance, sort through and get rid of articles that no longer fit anyone, others you don't like, and anything you have no intention of mending. For example, if you don't know how to put a fly zipper in, don't save pants that need this item replaced. Send them to charity, and let someone else repair them. Keep only clothing that will be serviceable and look nice after it is repaired.

Organize thread according to colors; do the same with bobbins. Storing thread and bobbins together rather than tossing bobbins in with machine attachments is a long-range time saver. Grouping thread according to purpose is also helpful. (For example, we have hand-quilting thread, machine-embroidery thread, buttonhole twist, and invisible hemming thread. All this was hard to keep track of when mixed in with general-purpose thread. Grouping threads was a big help.)

After evaluating your sewing notions, group the keepers together according to kind and store each group in its own container. Baby food jars, bouillon cube containers, even plastic sandwich bags make good containers for grouped sewing notions.

Simplify your zipper collection, too, and put what's left in labeled plastic zip-locked bags or some other container; sort the zippers according to length and kind. The entire assortment could then be stored in another labeled container. Be practical with zippers. We used to buy our notions in bulk at a sewing outlet, where zippers were so many cents a pound. Because they were such a fantastic buy, we'd buy anything and everything. So we ended up with placket zippers when what we needed were dress or skirt zippers, heavy-duty metal-toothed zippers that could hold a tank together when what we needed were plastic-toothed all-purpose zippers. These great buys lived in sewing areas for years, never earning their keep.

Treat buttons the same way as zippers; separate colors and kinds into zip-locked bags or glass jars. Make sure you are keeping only what you need and like. Remember, buttons tend to look dated and shoddy in less time than other sewing notions.

Any professional seamstress will tell you that careful attention to detail is what gives a home-sewn garment a professional look. Trims, such as piping, help with this look. Wrap and secure lace and trims around small cardboard pieces and store them in a container such as a shoebox. This eliminates messy tangles. You'll need a convenient place for all these notion containers, and if you don't have an accommodating sewing cabinet, you'll need a cupboard or shelved closet handy to your sewing spot.

Make your own piping by cutting 1½"-1¾" bias strips. Lay the cording vertically down the middle of the bias strips and fold right sides of fabric over the cording. (Cording can even be double strands of acrylic yarn.) Using a zipper foot, stitch fabric lengths, keeping the zipper foot as close to the cording as possible.

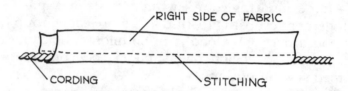

RIGHT SIDE OF FABRIC

CORDING   STITCHING

SAVE YOUR SEWING EQUIPMENT

Sewing equipment deserves proper care and maintenance. Routine oiling (if yours is the type that needs it), dusting, and cleaning are the keys to keeping your machine operating properly longer. Fabric scissors need regular sharpening—and be sure to use them only on fabric. (Other family members may not respect this rule, so the scissors may be better off hidden away from harm's reach.) Throw away all dull and bent pins and needles—don't even save them for the bulletin board—the next time you cut out a pattern, you will thank yourself.

If your sewing area is large enough, consider storing and using the ironing board there. When it's not in use, it could be tucked away onto a door-mount caddy.

Sewing is easier and more fun in a well-lighted, cheerful spot. A good sewing lamp is as important as a good machine, as helpful to the appearance of the finished product as a sharp needle. So if you don't already have good lighting, put a clamp-light on your want list.

Last but not really least, a bulletin board hung by the sewing machine is a great place to post instructions, sewing ideas, the repair shop number, and so on.

You'll find there's nothing more inviting than a simplified, orderly sewing area—it makes you love sewing all the more.

15

Not So
Behind-the-Scenes:
The Back Porch
or Deck

You know the typical back porch or deck—no matter what the size or shape, they have a few things in common. They're adjacent to an entrance and are an informal introduction to the house. They're part of a traffic pattern, often a busy one. They're often dirty and hard to keep clean. They tend to be catch-alls. Frequently, they're cluttered with unrelated items. Little or no thought is given to their arrangement, function, or purpose. They're often unattractive. They can be embarrassing, irritating, and bothersome.

All the same, another outside entrance to the house is a valuable amenity. It's worth having, so don't try to ignore it—instead, fix it up.

An ideal back porch or deck is functional, clean, and easy to keep that way. Whether yours consists of no more than cement steps or a cement slab, or is more elaborate—say, a glassed-in room or a wooden deck—achieving the ideal is possible.

First, carefully assess what you have to work with. Here are some ideas that will help you transform the bothersome into the ideal:

● Apply concrete sealer to any cement work. Porous concrete traps dirt and dust like a sponge and "bleeds," so after sweeping, soil is still there, looking ugly and waiting to be tracked in. Sealer eliminates the bleeding problem and makes the sweeping routine an easy one.

● Hang as much as possible. (If you have a closed-in back porch or deck, this could be a spot to hang up the broom, mop, and dustpan, or to accommodate a paper bag holder, maybe even the fly swatter.) The wall along a deck is usually the back of the house. This could support a few hanging things, such as a drawstring bag containing the barbeque utensils.

● Don't allow this area to be used as an annex to the garage. Yard and garden tools often end up on the back porch or deck because people don't take the time to put them away. Someone gases up the lawn mower, sets the gas can

143

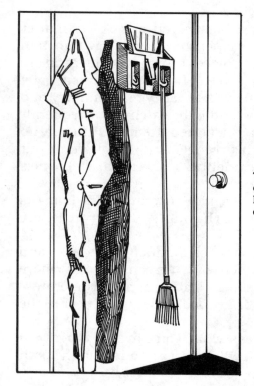

Take advantage of space in an enclosed back porch or deck to hang your broom and dustpan.

on the back porch, and there it stays. If you have no garage, don't allow this area to look like a makeshift garage. There is *always* another place for things, even if it's a metal shed, old school lockers, large wooden box, and so on. (If there's not a proper place for something, create one; if you can't, the "something" probably ought to go.)

• Make the back porch or deck a pleasant place to spend time. Consider putting potted plants, comfortable lawn furniture, a picnic table, a hammock, or whatever suits your fancy (and your space) out there. If your family likes to barbeque, perhaps you'd like to build a fire pit in the backyard. (For complete how-to instructions, see the Back-of-the-Book Bonuses section.)

• If there's no other place to store your lawn furniture during the off-season, then perhaps the wooden deck will be your spot. If it's the fold-up-style furniture, consider covering it with large plastic trash bags and hanging it where you can (on the back of the house, which would be one side of the deck, for example).

16

No More
No-Car Garage

onsider any ten homes on your block. Then ask yourself how many of the occupants can get their car into their garage. Although the original purpose of the garage is for parking your car, many people use it for indiscriminate storage, too. The garage is often treated as a warehouse; what can't fit into the house will surely fit into the garage. This results in piles of unused and unwanted stuff, all to be dealt with later. Only "later" never does come and the garage gets deeper and deeper in stuff. The garage becomes so overloaded that instead of being a one- or two-car garage, it becomes a no-car garage.

A no-car garage most likely stores unused and unwanted items.

Digging out a garage is easier if you do it in warm weather and allow yourself two days to complete the job. Use the usual key questions and techniques to decide what to keep and what to toss. When you are finished, the garage should be completely emptied and you should be dealing with only keeper piles. (Incidentally, this is an excellent time to seal the garage floor. Don Aslett's *Is There Life After Housework?* has more on this. After you have sealed this floor, it is easy to maintain with an industrial-size dust mop.)

Because the garage is an area where you don't have to be concerned with design and decor, you will be able to use walls and ceilings for hanging most things that are still stored in the garage. But keep in mind that things stored in the garage need protection from dust and dirt. (Drawstring bags or plastic garbage sacks are great for this.)

The way to get the most out of garage space is to designate separate areas for work and activity centers. Here are some typical centers:

- Car care center
- Tool and building supply center
- Yard and garden center
- Activity center (bikes and outside toys such as swimming or wading pool and sandbox toys go here)
- Barbeque center
- Camping equipment center
- Sports equipment center for all seasons
- Pet center
- Storage center

How often you use these centers will determine where to place them in your garage. For example, if you are an avid camper but leave your car maintenance to a professional mechanic, then your camping equipment will be assigned a place for easy access and the car care center will not have priority space.

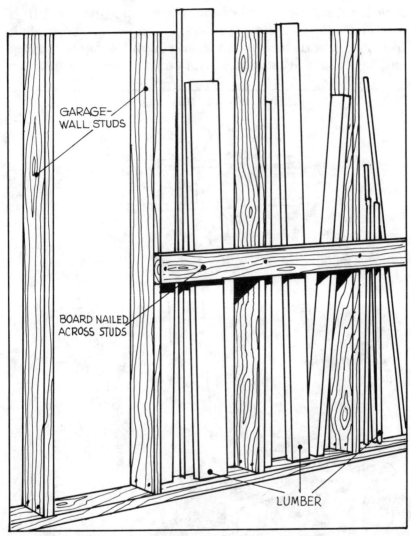

GARAGE-
WALL STUDS

BOARD NAILED
ACROSS STUDS

LUMBER

Store lumber behind a board nailed across garage-wall studs.

CAR CARE CENTER/
TOOL AND BUILDING-SUPPLY CENTER

Consider putting car-care equipment and other tools adjacent to each other for easy access. Getting as much as possible off the floor will keep you from tripping over things and enable you to keep the floor cleaner. To accomplish this, group and store like tools and supplies together. Keep smaller tools and supplies that cannot be hung in draw-

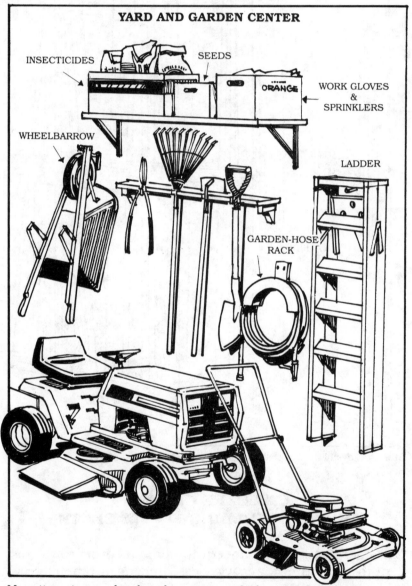

Many items in a yard and garden center can be hung or shelved.

ers. Store car care equipment and supplies in the same manner. For drawers, consider using an old dresser that is no longer welcome in the house.

Building supplies such as lumber can be stored between the studs of garage walls, with a small board nailed across to keep these supplies secure.

YARD AND GARDEN CENTER

Lawn mowers, snowblowers, and rototillers will occupy floor space. Hang shovels, rakes, trimmers, pruners, and so on from nails or on specially made tool racks, which are available in hardware stores. It's also worth investing in a garden hose rack. Ladders and wheelbarrows can also be hung for convenience.

Store all insecticides, sprays, or other chemicals in *labeled* containers on shelves out of reach of children. Put smaller items such as garden gloves and sprinklers in a labeled container for quick retrieval. These items can also be hung up in drawstring bags.

Although logic would have you store your garden seed with the yard and garden supplies, prudence advises against it. Temperature extremes in the garage aren't good for seed: chances of germination are lessened and deterioration is hastened. So keep garden seeds in a labeled, airtight container (glass canning jars are good) in your inside storage area.

Fine garden seed, such as carrot seed, can be mixed with sand or garden loam in a proportion of one pack of seed to four cups of sand. Put this mixture in a container with a pour spout, such as a half-gallon milk carton; shake it well to disperse the seed throughout the sand. Plant the seed by slowly pouring the mixture from the container down the row. Or broadcast the seed from this container onto the seed bed. The sand is an automatic thinning aid.

Options for containers in a recycling center include trash bags, wooden bins, and trash cans. Keep your recycling center in the garage or storage shed.

If recycling is part of your lifestyle, avoid the clutter and confusion it can cause by setting up your own mini-recycling center. Have a clearly labeled container for each category being saved. These containers could be metal or plastic trash cans, heavy-duty plastic trash bags, wooden bins, fifty-five gallon drums, even sturdy large cardboard boxes. Crushed aluminum cans, since they are light-weight, can be saved in a hanging bag. Newspapers, glass, and other metal will probably need floor space, however. Visit your local recycling center on a regular basis to keep this area under control.

Keep garage-stored firewood in bounds by stacking it in a rack or frame. A separate container of kindling is an added convenience. In parts of the country where termites are a problem, people are strongly advised to store wood *outside* the house or garage; if you live in this kind of region, you can still keep your wood neat by storing it in a rack or frame.

To avoid tracking dirt from outside to inside, assign a place to hang outside work clothes and shoes. If you want garbage cans in the garage, get them off the floor by using a wall-hung rack or frame. Attach a chain or rope to the side supports and draw it across the front of the cans to keep them upright. You can attach this rack to the outside of a garage wall if you prefer.

ACTIVITY CENTER

Outside toys need adequate storage space. Many items, such as a small wading pool, bike training wheels, or bike tire pump, can be hung. Provide shelves for toy trucks, cars, scoop shovels, and other sandbox toys. Avoid using an open box for toy storage—this invites indiscriminate tossing, chucking, and stuffing.

Large hooks attached to the eaves provide an imaginative solution to bicycle storage.

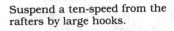

Suspend a ten-speed from the rafters by large hooks.

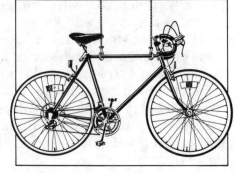

There are various ways to store bikes. Ten-speeds can be stored on a rack made from two-by-fours notched to support cross bars. Large sturdy hooks on rafters or walls also can store bikes. One family we know even stores their bikes during winter on large hooks under the eaves of their home, outside their garage, away from the public view. Another idea is to construct a wrought-iron gate rack for bike storage. All you need to make this is a four-foot section of porch railing, plus mounting hardware and some scrap lumber. The frame is made from two-by-fours lap-jointed at corners and screwed together. Another two-by-four joins the ends together to keep the structure rigid.

BARBEQUE CENTER

The style of your barbeque grill determines how you store it. Most grills on legs, and smaller hibachis, too, can be hung on hooks from rafters or walls. Propane grills are heavier and therefore difficult to hang, so they require floor space. Don't overlook the possibility of grouping barbeque utensils with the grill and storing them either inside the propane kind, in a plastic bag for cleanliness, or bagging them and hanging the bag alongside the grill. Store the charcoal and starter fluid there, too.

CAMPING EQUIPMENT CENTER

If you store this equipment in the garage, then store it properly, as described in Chapter 12: Consolidate, hang as much as possible, and keep it inventoried.

Consider storing the picnic jug, picnic tablecloth, perhaps even the picnic basket inside your camper cooler. We always keep extra paper plates plus paper-plate holders, cups, plastic utensils, matches, and a can opener in our picnic baskets. Some avid campers house all the cooking gear (pots, pans, griddle, utensils, dish soap, scouring pads, dish towels, dish cloths, and dish tub) in a wooden box with handles.

Tent campers can keep tent pegs, poles, whisk broom, and a sheathed hatchet inside a large duffle or drawstring bag made just for this purpose. Deflated air mattresses can be folded lengthwise in thirds, rolled up into small units, and secured with elastics. These can then be stored inside a specially marked drawstring bag and kept with the sleeping bags. If you use foam mattresses under your sleeping bags, they can be rolled into tight cylinders, secured with cord, popped into drawstring bags, and hung up as well.

This is also the center where the tackle box, fishing poles (in a tube container), reels, catch bag, and rubber waders would go.

We know of one camping center so efficiently set up that it has individual backpacks, loaded and ready for travel, hung up in dust covers along the top of a garage wall beside the shelved picnic gear.

SPORTS EQUIPMENT CENTER

Most sports equipment can be hung, so designate specific wall space for this. (Good sports equipment is expensive: use drawstring bags or plastic garbage bags to protect it from dust and dirt.) The following equipment is especially suited to being hung, either loose or in containers:

√All balls and ball-related equipment—ball mitts and bats, ball shoes, knee pads, inflating needles (in their own small pouch inside the large bag), small bicycle pump.

√Swimming equipment—fins, goggles, nose and ear plugs, snorkles, deflated air mattresses and inner tubes, bundled in a durable drawstring bag.

√Snow ski equipment—ski poles, snow boots, goggles, ski wax, ski gloves, ski hats, ski thermals (with smaller items grouped together in drawstring bags).

√Croquet sets and golf clubs, *if* you use a sturdy hook and cover the equipment with a plastic bag.

√Tennis and badminton racquets—hang related balls and birdies in a bag.

155

√Sleds.

√Bicycles.

√Stilts and pogo sticks.

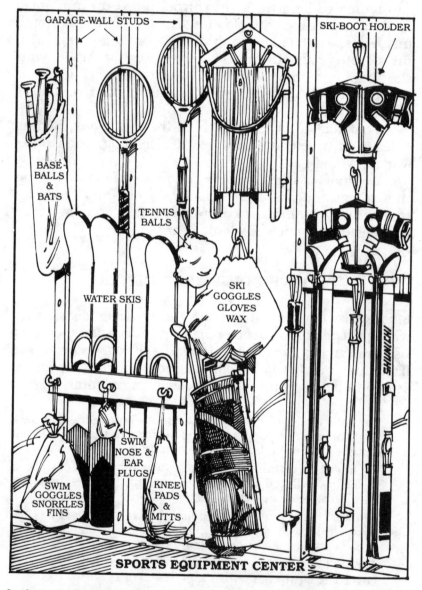

In this sports equipment center, small pieces of equipment are stored in hanging drawstring bags.

156

PET CENTER

Pet food and supplies need to be stored in a place that is easy to keep clean. If your garage is attached or handy to your home, consider putting this area near the garage door so it can be hosed down for easier maintenance. But if your garage is well removed from your home, then consider setting up a feeding station near your back door. To help avoid spills and for easier dispensing, put dry cat food into an empty gallon plastic milk jug; a milk carton works well for large-chunked dog food, too. Keep a can opener, to be used for pet food only, near the pet food area, and place newspaper or a paper bag under the feeding bowls for snappy cleanup.

STORAGE CENTER

If you are without storage space inside the house, you're probably extra appreciative of your garage space, and a storage center there is a must. Designate a specific section of your garage for storage. Set this center up with durable shelving and heavy-duty hooks. Use the walls and ceiling to hang as much as possible. Protect stored items with dust covers. Be sure to group like categories together, and label containers for easy recognition of contents.

Here are a couple of "ultimates" in the way of garage storage that we've seen: One family partitioned off a 6' by 13' section, insulated it, installed a light, and equipped it with floor-to-ceiling shelves running down both 13' walls. With only a 30" walkway between shelved walls, you can imagine how much this partitioned area stores. Another family dedicated one entire garage wall (from floor to ceiling) to closets and cupboards. All doors can be locked and all closet/cupboard insides are lined with pegboard. The advantages of both systems are that the garage appears neater, the stored items are better protected, and enclosed spaces discourage random drop-offs (so things tend to be put back where they belong and spaces can fulfill their specific assignments).

17

That "Someplace Else": The Super Storage Area

When we discuss "storage area," we're referring to any spot that you've dedicated specifically to *storage*. This could be the attic, part of the basement, a section of the garage, a large closet (or several closets), a backyard shed, or even an away-from-home rental unit.

Actually, the kind of storage area we're talking about in this chapter should not be a "someplace else," but it is too often treated as if it were. When we can't decide where something goes, we just put it someplace—and that someplace is the storage area. And several years of storage shoving is bad news, for you and the storage.

When it comes to overload, the storage area is usually one of the worst cases. If you've been even a sometime storage-shover, then you probably don't know what's in there or where it is.

Wasted space, often caused by saving duplicates, is another problem the average storage area faces. Old loose-leaf binders, bathroom hardware, toilet tank lids, broken TVs, and so on, eat up precious space.

This area is probably holding some dead storage, too. Dead storage is what has been forgotten, untouched, unused, unopened. We know many homemakers who have boxes in their storage area that have never been opened—they stay sealed from move to move. One typical dead storage item is hand-me-down clothes. We store and store them but seldom wear them; they get buried and forgotten. When they're finally discovered, everyone has outgrown them. Everything in storage should be "alive," waiting to go into service, rather than dead and waiting to go to the garbage or local charity.

Alive and not dead, efficient and not full—that's a professional storage area. And an efficient and professional storage area is a back-up system for the entire home. A home back-up system anticipates needs and is prepared to meet them. For instance, we eventually run out of toilet paper, plastic wrap, toothpaste, cellophane tape, dishwasher detergent, and so on. We periodically need to replace lightbulbs, vacuum belts and bags, furnace filters, car oil, and so on. A back-up system holds replacements for all these items.

A good storage area is also a holding area for all temporarily inactive keepers. For instance, although you may not need them now, you may eventually need the crib bumpers, bassinet, and high chair back in service. The same goes for good hand-me-downs. Suitcases are another "temporarily inactive" group.

This holding area keeps temporarily inactive items out of the active main flow of the home. It provides orderly, efficient protection for things that are waiting for their term of service.

Deal with this spot as you did the kitchen, emptying it all out, putting the contents in related piles. Work through the piles until only keepers are left. Then designate centers in your storage area according to available space and keeper categories. Your categories of keeper piles automatically determine your centers.

Basically, there are two types of storage: seasonal-occasional, and home management. A single storage area can efficiently house both types if specific centers are designated. If you have loads of storage space, you could split the two categories up, sending one type to one area and the other type to another area. However you do it, the point is to carefully assess all intended storage items, evaluate and assign specific spots to each storage category, and group and store like items together.

Notice how supermarkets group and store like items together, often stocking from the floor to the ceiling. This type of storage uses space efficiently, and it adapts well to home storage areas.

SEASONAL-OCCASIONAL STORAGE

This is what the name implies—things used only seasonally or occasionally. These things aren't used often enough to merit prime space in the rest of the house, so they're assigned to the storage area. Some possible examples: canning equipment, sports equipment, holiday decorations, summer wear and beach towels, picnic and camping supplies, suitcases, turkey roaster, good hand-me-downs, quilting frames and stands, old college textbooks. The garage, basement, crawl space, attic, and shed are obvious places for this type of storage. What if you don't have spaces like that available? You could convert a typical linen closet into a storage area, or install floor-to-ceiling shelves in a portion of a clothes closet. Stay away from under-the-bed storage, though.

There are some things you can do to maximize your space and increase your storing efficiency. Use all available space within the area by hanging as much as possible. For example, bag and hang spare bath and bed linens; do the same for sleeping bags and extra toys. Almost anything with a handle or a hole in it can be hung: turkey roaster (with the baster inside), Christmas tree stand, high chair, card table and folding chairs, even the movie projector screen. (You may need to tie a rope through some of these handles or holes for easier hanging.)

Consolidation is another space saver. Many suitcase sets can be packed inside one another: the tote bag inside the small case, and then the small case inside the large. The bassinet could hold a drawstring bag or box of baby clothes or diapers, baby room decor items, or perhaps a bag of baby toys. Then, of course, hang these groups of consolidated items up.

Be creative with your shelving. Besides the assembled metal shelves and traditional wooden shelves, you can use boards laid across cement blocks, storage buckets, bricks—even filled gallon jars can support shelf boards.

To keep control of this area, always consider the purpose of things, where they are used, and how often they are used—then put things where they belong. We remember seeing a storage area littered with used toilet seats and old plumbing fixtures. The owner of all this also owned a few rental units. Since he was sure he'd need these things as replacements, it made good sense to keep them, he thought. We suggested this collection be stored at the rental units, thus freeing space and giving him more control of his storage area.

Don't be tempted to just shove things into the storage area until you can find someplace else for them. Get in the habit of practicing on-the-spot assessment: make immediate decisions and you'll avoid overloaded spaces.

HOME-MANAGEMENT STORAGE

Again, this is just what the name implies—back-up supplies of anything used in managing the home (toilet paper, dish, bath and laundry soaps, grooming and hygiene products, plastic wrap, paper towels, and so on).

The garage is an adequate place for this, but it has its drawbacks: It gets dirty easily and is hard to clean, and it is subject to temperature extremes which shorten shelf life. Garage storage calls for careful packaging and pest-proof containers, more so than house storage. Sometimes the garage is inconveniently located. Remember, too, that cement floors sweat and can rust metal containers and deteriorate paper and cardboard. That means you'll need to lay down wooden slats before you do floor stacking. Don't put off organizing your storage because you need boards cut and laid. It's no big deal to get this done—just measure the length you need and go get the boards. Lumber yard and home improvement center people are very accommodating. They'll cut your lengths for you. Then just lay the slats down and load your storage area.

The garage is better than nothing, though, and you can improve a garage storage situation by framing a portion in and insulating it, creating a mini-storage room.

Beneath-the-house crawl space will work, too, even if the floor is dirt (although you'll need wooden slats then, too). We've seen some very ingenious ideas in the crawl space, from short shelving to floor-joist hanging. Many things can be put in drawstring bags and hung from the floor joists. It's not necessary to give shelf space to items like first-aid supplies, garden seeds, candles, matches, grooming and hygiene products, sewing notions, light bulbs, and so on. Even five-gallon buckets or water jugs can be hung if the nails are strong, hammered in far enough, and put in at a severe angle.

Above-the-house crawl space, or the attic, will work like your beneath-the-house crawl space. Only in this case your hanging will be done from roof trusses or rafters. The major drawback here is like the garage—the temperature extremes must be worked around.

Although it is true that storage isn't used as much if it's hard to get to, it's also true that you'll be more inclined to use it if it is stocked in an efficient, orderly way. With thoughtful planning, even attic or crawl space storage can be made workable.

Another good storage spot is the hall linen closet spoken of earlier. Empty it out completely and assign each shelf specific categories.

We can't overlook the basement as a natural storage center. Whether you use just a section of it or devote the entire area to storage, be sure to have a specific plan for placing your categories of things—don't just cram and stuff things here and there. If yours is a concrete floor, you would also benefit from sealing it with the aforementioned concrete sealer and then laying down wooden slats before doing stacking.

Here are some basic tips for stocking and maintaining a home-management storage area that is a living asset to your home rather than a graveyard of dead stuff.

- As always, group and store like items together, just as the grocery store does; don't scatter.
- Consolidate as much as possible.

> To transfer dry items such as detergent or pet food into other containers, cut the bottom off a large paper grocery sack. Then insert it into the mouth of a gallon jar or other small-mouthed container. Spread it apart at the bottom, fan it out at the top, and use as a giant funnel.

- Assign a specific space for empties. No more setting empty gallon jars, five-gallon buckets, or drawstring bags on a shelf in front of full containers.
- Hang as much as possible.
- Use the grocery store arrangement by lining the perimeter of your area with shelving, then run stacks of shelves both parallel and perpendicular to this. This method is intended for an actual storage room, but it can also work in a crawl space, as it does for Alice.
- Use an inventory system: Consistently record what you have, how much you have, and where it is; other pertinent information is date of purchase, date opened, expiration date. Inventorying is one of the main reasons for making your storage convenient. If you can't get to it, you won't rotate it or inventory it.
- Store what your family uses and likes, and use what you store. Alice found a fantastic buy on an off-brand toothpaste. No wonder it was such a great buy—it tasted like white glue. Her family detested it and refused to use it. So her wonderful bargain sat, taking up precious space. She finally chucked it. She discovered that the biggest expense was not in the money she paid for it, but rather in the space she gave to storing it.

An efficient, convenient, well-stocked storage area can mean the difference between just getting by and enjoying comfort and your usual standard of living indefinitely. It is also a great hedge against inflation and a source of peace of mind. It's not just a "someplace else."

Conclusion:
It Really Is Here . . .
Somewhere

It really is here . . . somewhere! Not only the end of the book, but the beginning of an improved lifestyle. No more creeping, growing clutter; no more bulging closets, cupboards, and drawers; no more time wasted doing the household shuffle. No more excuses; no more frustration. Now *you* are in control, truly a professional homemaker.

As you're enjoying this constant order and control, remember one thing: bad habits die hard. Because they're tough to kill, you must be even tougher in your persistence at establishing good ones. Don't give in to the old ways of managing (or mismanaging) your home; stick with your streamlining as a lifestyle. And don't let a little backsliding by you or others discourage you. It'll happen once in a while, but it's nothing to panic over, because you can recapture order as quickly as it was lost.

Remember, also, that success in anything, including homemaking, is a combination of having the right attitudes, the right principles, the right strategies, and the right techniques, and then being willing to pay the price. Instead of settling into that crowded comfort zone populated by those who resist change, step out—stick with this better system of homemaking. Simply do it.

Back-of-the-Book Bonuses

HOOK IT
(Using standard screw-in hooks, nails, eye bolts)

THE MANY LIVES OF A DRAWSTRING BAG

HOW TO MAKE DRAWSTRING BAGS—
THE STREAMLINED WAY

HOW TO MAKE A CLOSET LAUNDRY BAG

HOW TO BUILD A FIRE PIT

HOOK IT
(Using standard screw-in hooks, nails, eye bolts)

AREA	WHERE	WHAT
Kitchen	behind refrigerator or underneath an above-the-refrigerator cupboard	broom, dust pan, mop, whisk broom
	underside of countertops (at end of bank of cupboards)	phone book, calendar
	on inside of cupboard doors and walls; underside of cupboard shelves	large plastic bowl, colander, dish drainer tray (with hole in one end and string tied through for loop), turkey roaster, pots and pans, utensils, appliance cords (wound and secured), measuring cups, grater, bag and wrap holder, cleaning-supplies holder, trash holder
Garage or Outside Storage Shed	walls/studs; ceiling joists; undersides of shelves	bikes, barbeque grills, stroller, car seat, ladders, wheelbarrow, garden tools, fertilizer spreader, yard equipment, camping equipment, kiddie wading pool, lawn chairs, spare carpet rolls, hibachi, spare tires/snow tires, hand tools, suitcases, saddles and bridles

NOTE: Certain items will store better and be easier to maintain if slipped into a large plastic bag (such as a trash bag) before hanging.

THE MANY LIVES OF A DRAWSTRING BAG

AREA	WHERE	WHAT
Kitchen	inside cupboard doors; inside cupboard walls; underneath cupboard shelves; underneath sink from underside of kitchen countertop	dry packaged mixes, extension and appliance cords, cleaning supplies and equipment, matches, lamp wicks, candles, cookie cutters, birthday cake candles and cake decorations, tool kit, shoeshine kit, pastas, dry beans, and seeds
Bathroom	inside vanity doors; underneath sink, along inside vanity walls; underneath sink from underside of vanity top; inside cupboard doors and walls	curlers, curling irons, blow dryers and attachments, hair clippers and attachments, makeup, feminine hygiene needs, bar soaps, other toiletries, extra towel set
Bedrooms	in closets along perimeter walls and underside of closet shelf; from closet ceiling; along a "hook board" on wall	toys, games, shoes, boots, sleeping bags, belts, extra bed linens, child's "treasure collection," scarves, jewelry, makeup, purses (for dust protection)
Closets	on back side of hinged door; along inside walls: from underneath closet shelf; from closet ceiling; from closet rod	seasonal sporting goods (ski accessories, soccer equipment), cold-weather outerwear (hats, mittens, gloves, boots), shoeshine kits, cleaning supplies/ tools, film and cameras, medicines, school supplies, sewing notions, lightbulbs, oil and acrylic paint tubes with brushes, extra toys, spare bed and bath linens
Storage	from ceiling; from underside of shelves; from back of solid doors; from ceiling or floor joists (in the case of crawl space); along walls	candles/matches/lamp wicks, seasonal items (holiday decorations), sewing notions, fabric, infant seat (for dust protection), flavorings, herbs, spices, bar soaps, toiletries (disposable razors, toothbrushes, toothpaste), school supplies, canning booklets/ equipment
Garage	ceiling joists; wall studs; from underside of shelves	camping equipment, sports equipment, seasonal items (barbeque utensils, yard toys), pet supplies, garden seeds, small garden tools and gloves, sleeping bags

HOW TO MAKE DRAWSTRING BAGS—THE STREAMLINED WAY

The purpose of the bag determines your choice of fabric.

The purpose of the bag determines its width and length.

The type of drawstring used determines the casing width.

Drawstring suggestions: shoelaces, bias tape, heavy string, jute, macramé cord, chalk line, old drapery cording.

Allow ½" seams.

To "mass-produce" drawstring bags:

1. Sew a tube, right sides together, the width of the finished bag plus seam allowance, and the length equaling the number of bags times their length plus the bottom seam allowances.

   Width equation: bag width + ½" seam allowance
   Length equation: (number of bags × bag length) + (number of bags × seam allowance)

   Example: 4 bags, 12" wide, 14" long
   width = 12" + ½" = 12½" wide
   length = (4 bags x 14") + (4 bags × ½") = (56") + (2") = 58" long

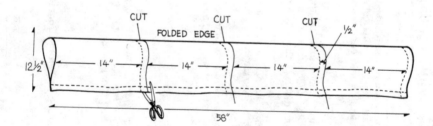

2. Stitch across the width of the tube at intervals equaling the desired bag length.

3. Cut across the tube ½" from each line of stitches.

4. Measure drawstrings for each bag. Each string should measure twice the bag width plus two inches. Example: (12" × 2) + 2" = 24" + 2" = 26" of string per bag.

5. Fasten each string into an approximate 24" loop, using an overhand knot.

6. Put the bag, still right sides together, up through this looped string.

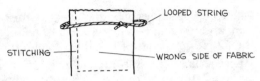

7. Fold the raw edge down over the drawstring, making the casing wide enough to allow stitching in place without catching the cord.

8. Cut small slits in the casing on each side of bag to allow the drawstring to be pulled through.

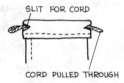

9. Finally, turn the bag right side out and pull up the drawstrings.

HOW TO MAKE A CLOSET LAUNDRY BAG

Use a sturdy wooden hanger. Its width will determine the width of the finished bag. The length of the finished bag is up to you.

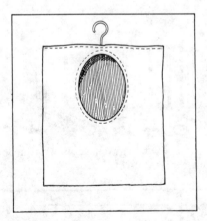

Instructions:
1. Measure two pieces of fabric the desired width and length.
2. In one piece, cut a large circle or oval opening. Finish and reinforce this opening with bias tape.

3. Place the right sides of both pieces together and sew side, bottom, and top seams, leaving a small opening in the middle of the top seam to allow the hanger to slip through.

4. Turn the bag right-side-out and insert the hanger through the opening. (It can be removed when you launder the bag.)

Note: A pillowcase works well for this project, also. Cut the circle in one side, finishing with bias tape. Stitch along the opening of the case, leaving a space for the hanger insertion.

HOW TO BUILD A FIRE PIT

A backyard fire pit is a great place for family fun and informal get-togethers—roasting hot dogs, summer night singalongs, and so on. A grill can be put across the hole for barbequing, and three Dutch ovens will fit into the pit for delicious Dutch oven meals. If you'd like to try your hand at building a brick fire pit, here's how:

Needed: Approximately 43 fire bricks/shovel/hand trowel

1. Dig a straight-sided hole approximately three feet in diameter. The length of your fire brick determines the depth of the hole.

2. Line the side walls of the pit with bricks placed on end, packing soil tightly around each brick to secure it in place. The tops of the vertical bricks should sit flush with the grass around the top of the hole.

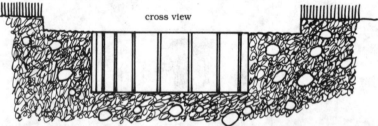
cross view

3. Cut a strip of soil and grass as wide as the length of firebricks, away from mouth of pit:

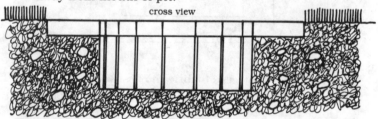
cross view

4. Lay fire bricks flat in the cut-away area, fairly close together, around the mouth of the pit. Pack tightly with soil. Grass will grow back quickly and fill in spaces. (Bricks should be flush with or slightly below grass line to allow for easy mowing.)

5. Do not line the bottom of pit with bricks; leave the soil floor to permit sufficient drainage.

top view

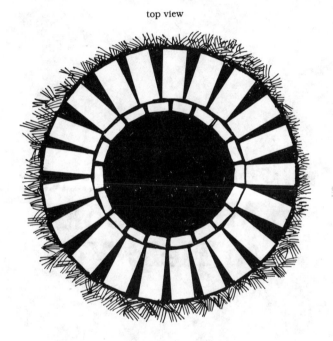

Suggested Reading:
More Books
to Help You

Aslett, Don. *Clutter's Last Stand.* Cincinnati: Writer's Digest Books, 1984. Using anecdotes, cartoons, quizzes, and "bumper snickers," Aslett shows how to uncover junk areas (from the basement to food), judge junk, and decide what we really *should* keep.

Aslett, Don. *Is There Life After Housework?* Cincinnati: Writer's Digest Books, 1985. Aslett shows how to save up to 75 percent of the time you spend housecleaning by using the tools and techniques of professional cleaners. Includes charts, diagrams, and step-by-step instructions for cleaning windows, carpets, furniture, and more.

Dorff, Pat. *File . . . Don't Pile.* Minneapolis: Willowtree Press, 1983. Pat Dorff is a professional librarian, lecturer, and consultant, as well as the creator of the "File . . . Don't Pile" workshop. Her unique filing system is now available in book form. (Send inquiries to Willowtree Press, Inc., 8108 33rd Pl. N., Minneapolis, MN 55427.)

Fjelstul, Alice Bancroft, Patricia Shad, and Barbara Marhoefer. *Early American Wall Stencils in Color.* New York: E.P. Dutton, 1982. Featured are step-by-step directions for stenciling walls and fabrics, as well as more than seventy-five full-sized stencil patterns. In our opinion, this is the last word on the subject!

McCullough, Bonnie. *Bonnie's Household Organizer.* New York: St. Martin's Press, 1980. This book won't make you rich, and it won't make your work go away. What it will do, if you have a desire to improve your efficiency, is help you get organized so that you can get done what needs to be done and go on to other things.

McCullough, Bonnie, and Susan Monson. *401 Ways to Get Your Kids to Work at Home.* New York: St. Martin's Press, 1982. This book has the answers and ideas to the age-old problem of getting children to be more responsible and help more with family living. This book is a fantastic companion volume to *It's Here . . . Somewhere!*

Schofield, Deniece. *Confessions of a Happily Organized Family.* Cincinnati: Writer's Digest Books, 1984. Schofield's hundreds of practical ideas will make mornings more peaceful, chores more fun, and mealtime a relaxing family affair.

Schofield, Deniece. *Confessions of an Organized Housewife.* Cincinnati: Writer's Digest Books, 1981. Schofield shares her energy-efficient system for organizing time, the kitchen, paperwork, laundry, storage areas, toys—the entire house.

Index

Other Home & Family Books of Interest

Confessions of a Happily Organized Family, by Deniece Schofield—How to work together as a family to restore (or establish!) a comfortable sense of order to your home. You'll find specific techniques for making mornings less hectic, traveling with kids, making chores fun, and more. 246 pages, $7.95, paper.

Confessions of an Organized Houswife, by Deniece Schofield—Schofield shares her secrets of household organization and time management, with specific ideas for organizing every aspect of home life—the kitchen, laundry, paperwork, storage areas, and more—to help you take control of your life! 214 pages, $6.95, paper

Is There Life After Housework?, by Don Aslett—America's #1 Cleaning Expert shows you how to save up to 75% of the time you now spend cleaning your home by using the tools and techniques the professionals use. 178 pages, $7.95, paper

Do I Dust or Vacuum First?, by Don Aslett—Here are answers to the 100 most-often-asked housecleaning questions, including how to keep your no-wax floors looking like new and how to clean brick walls. 183 pages, $6.95, paper

Clutter's Last Stand, by Don Aslett—In this "ultimate self-improvement book," Aslett gives you the courage to sift, sort, and toss whatever is detrimental to your housekeeping (and mental!) health—and get rid of clutter once and for all. 276 pages, $8.95, paper

Teach Me Mommy, by Jill Dunford—This preschool home learning guide is filled with fully-developed activities, complete with suggested books to read to the children, songs, crafts, and even treats to make together—all organized into 24 "theme" units. A great way to spend quality time with your kids while preparing them for the day they start school. 290 pages, $11.95, paper

Extra Cash for Women, by Susan Gillenwater & Virginia Dennis—Turn your talent, creativity, and energy into extra income with this guide to scores of home-based jobs. Includes tips on how to raise start-up money, advertise your business, and win your family's support. 312 pages, $8.95, paper

Extra Cash for Kids, by Larry Belliston & Kurt Hanks—Kids 8-16 will find more than 100 ways to earn money during summer and spare-time hours, with complete details on how to do the job, equipment needed, and pricing. 185 pages, $6.95, paper

USE THIS COUPON TO ORDER YOUR COPIES TODAY!

_ _

YES! Please send me the following books:

_____ (1145) Confessions of a Happily Organized Family, $7.95 ea.

_____ (1143) Confessions of an Organized Housewife, $6.95 ea.

_____ (1455) Is There Life After Housework?, $7.95 ea.

_____ (1214) Do I Dust or Vacuum First?, $6.95 ea.

_____ (1122) Clutter's Last Stand, $8.95 ea.

_____ (2204) Teach Me Mommy, $11.95 ea.

_____ (1245) Extra Cash for Women, $8.95 ea.

_____ (1246) Extra Cash for Kids, $6.95 ea.

(Please add $2.00 postage & handling for one book, 50¢ for each additional book. Ohio residents add 5½% sales tax.)   1855

☐ Payment enclosed   Please charge my: ☐ Visa ☐ MasterCard

   Acct. # _____ Exp. Date __

   Signature _____

Name _____

Address _____

City _____ State _____ Zip _____

_ _

Send to: Writer's Digest Books, 9933 Alliance Road,
         Cincinnati, Ohio 45242